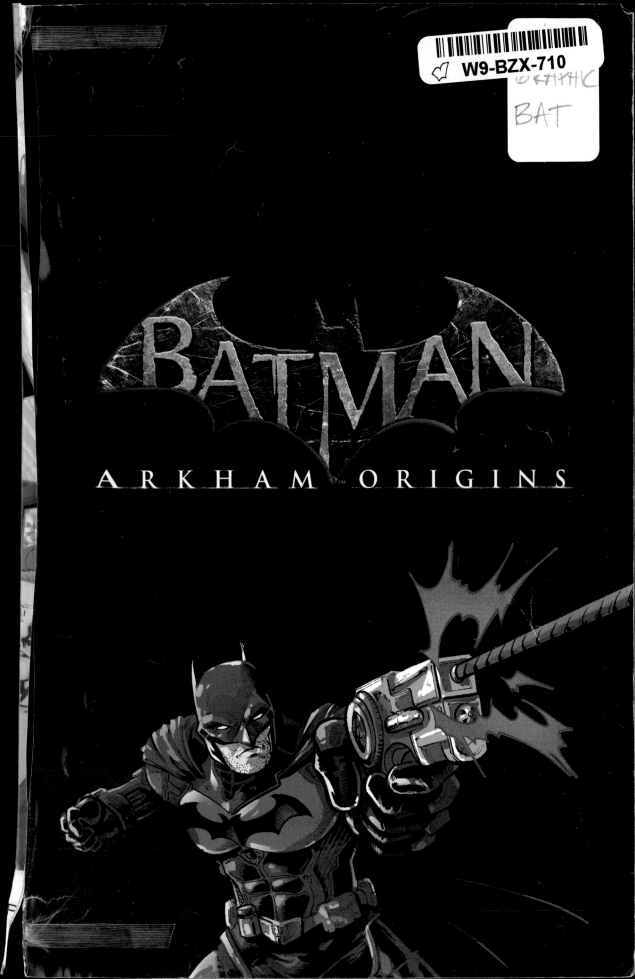

BATMAN

ARKHAM ORIGINS

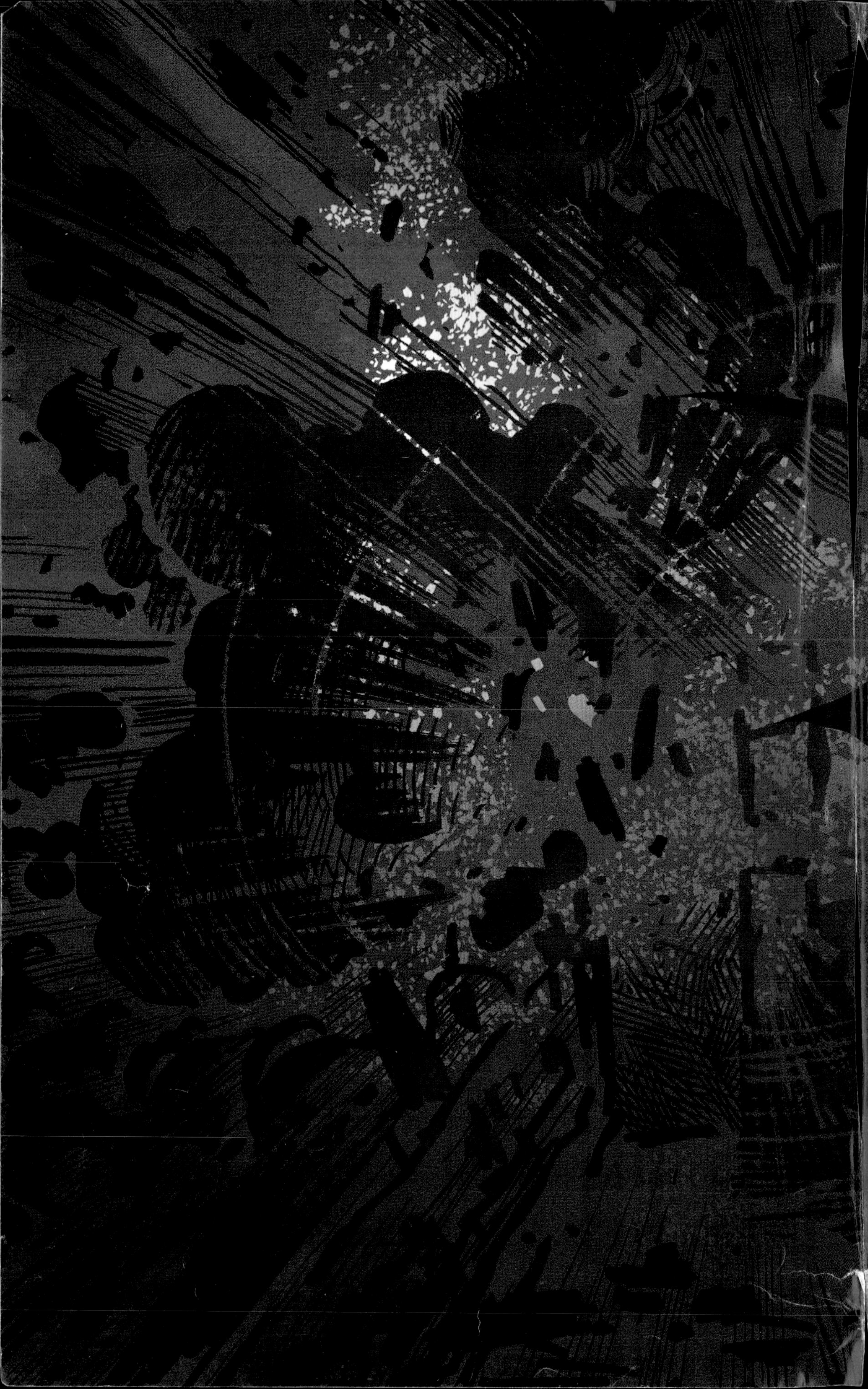

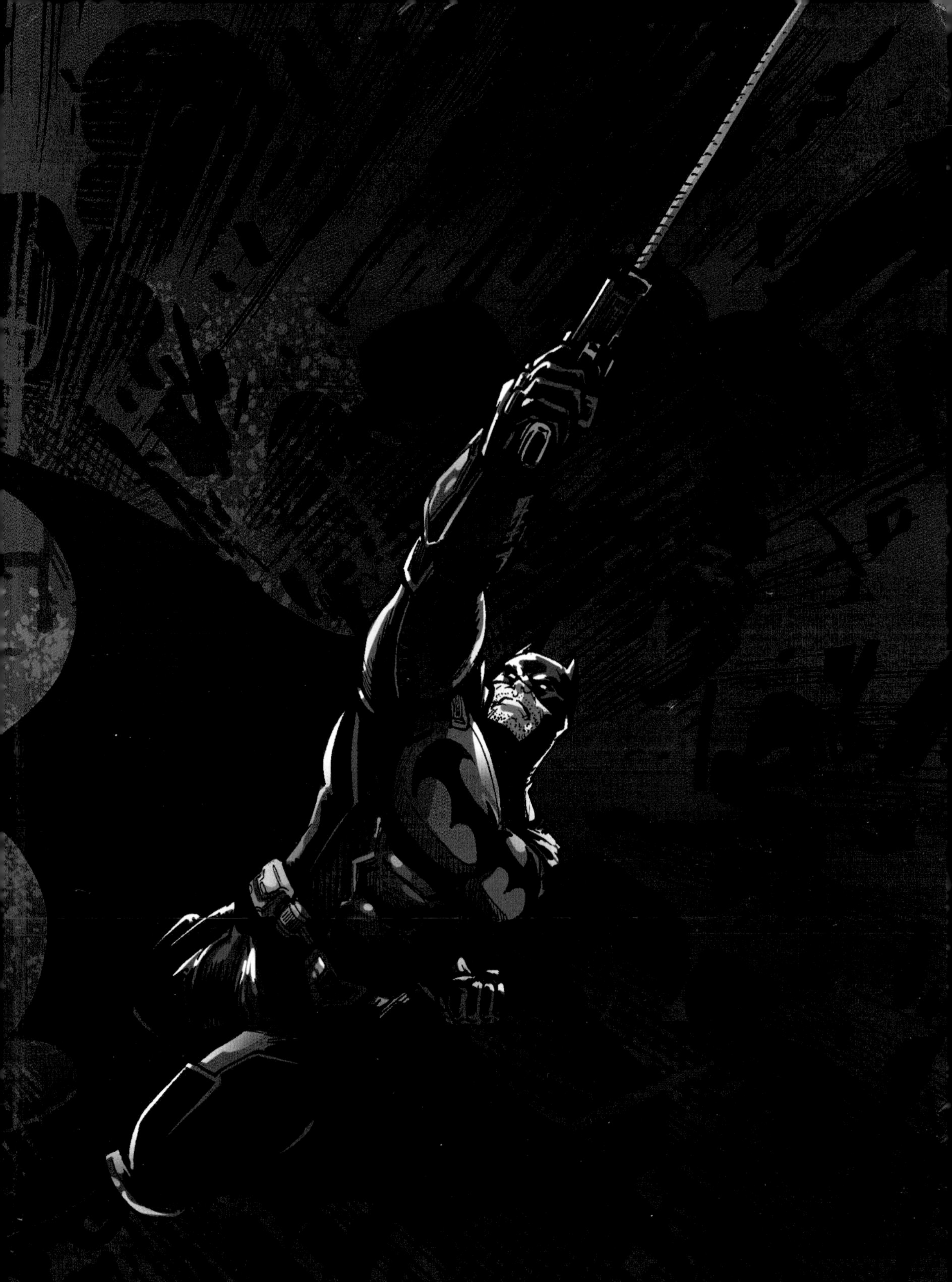

BATMAN: ARKHAM ORIGINS

Adam Beechen Plot Adam Beechen Doug Wagner Frank Hannah Script
Christian Duce Layouts Christian Duce Richard Ortiz Federico Dallocchio Vicente Cifuentes
Omar Francia Victor Drujiniu Thomas Derenick Finished Art
Santi Casas & David Lopez of Ikari Studio Colors
Travis Lanham Lettering Bryan Hitch with David Baron Collection Cover Artists
Batman created by Bob Kane

Jim Chadwick Editor – Original Series
Alex Antone Associate Editor – Original Series
Aniz Ansari Assistant Editor – Original Series
Peter Hamboussi Editor
Robbin Brosterman Design Director – Books
Louis Prandi Publication Design
Hank Kanalz Senior VP – Vertigo & Integrated Publishing
Diane Nelson President
Dan DiDio and Jim Lee Co-Publishers
Geoff Johns Chief Creative Officer
Amit Desai Senior VP – Marketing & Franchise Management
Amy Genkins Senior VP – Business & Legal Affairs
Nairi Gardiner Senior VP – Finance
Jeff Boison VP – Publishing Planning
Mark Chiarello VP – Art Direction & Design
John Cunningham VP – Marketing
Terri Cunningham VP – Editorial Administration
Larry Ganem VP – Talent Relations & Services
Alison Gill Senior VP – Manufacturing & Operations
Jay Kogan VP – Business & Legal Affairs, Publishing
Jack Mahan VP – Business Affairs, Talent
Nick Napolitano VP – Manufacturing Administration
Sue Pohja VP – Book Sales
Fred Ruiz VP – Manufacturing Operations
Courtney Simmons Senior VP – Publicity
Bob Wayne Senior VP – Sales

BATMAN: ARKHAM ORIGINS
Published by DC Comics. Cover and Compilation Copyright © 2015
DC Comics. Originally published online © 2013-2014. All Rights
Reserved. All characters, their distinctive likenesses and related
elements featured in this publication are trademarks of DC Comics.
The stories, characters and incidents featured in this publication are
entirely fictional. DC Comics does not read or accept unsolicited
ideas, stories or artwork.
DC Comics, 4000 Warner Blvd., Burbank, CA 91522
A Warner Bros. Entertainment Company.
Printed by RR Donnelley, Owensville, MO, USA.
5/29/15. First Printing.
ISBN 978-1-4012-5465-0

Library of Congress Cataloging-in-Publication Data

Beechen, Adam.
  Batman : Arkham origins / Adam Beechen, Doug Wagner.
    pages cm
  ISBN 978-1-4012-5465-0
  1. Graphic novels. I. Wagner, Doug, 1967- II. Title.
  PN6728.B36B56 2014
  741.5'973—dc23
               2014011700

SUSTAINABLE
FORESTRY
INITIATIVE

Certified Chain of Custody
20% Certified Forest Content,
80% Certified Sourcing
www.sfiprogram.org
SFI-01042
APPLIES TO TEXT STOCK ONLY

Introduction by Adam Beechen

"What is the future of comics?"

When people find out that I've done some work in the comics industry, it's a question I get fairly often. I don't pretend to have an Amulet of Nabu I can consult, or a Madame Xanadu I can call, to get information about the future, but it is something I've thought a good deal about.

There's been a lot of hand-wringing about what the Digital Age will "do" to comics. After all, we've seen the toll taken on newspapers, magazines and other print media. Adults can easily get their news, opinions, images and entertainment faster and in a wider variety than printed periodicals can provide them, from their phones, tablets, computers, televisions  and brain implants (if you're reading this after 2021). Kids, long the lifeblood of the comics industry, have more entertainment options than ever before, thanks to the meteoric rise of extreme sports, not to mention the light years video games have come since their earliest days (Can you imagine those poor, primitive Space Invaders unwittingly landing in the middle of a HALO firefight? Game over in five seconds).

What all these things – new and social media, extreme sports, video games – have in common is that they place the participant at the heart of the action. There's no such thing any longer as being on the outside looking in, not if we have a computer (and who doesn't – and will admit it?). We're at the center of it all, and we love it. We love that we don't have to take the news the local paper gives us once a day — we get to pick which sources of news we consume. We can share our pictures with everyone in the world if we want to, and (just about) no one can stop us. We love that we don't have to rely on a DJ to provide the music he thinks we should hear – we can select our own. In our games, we love that we get to decide which hallway to walk down, what accessories to carry, and where to aim our weapon.

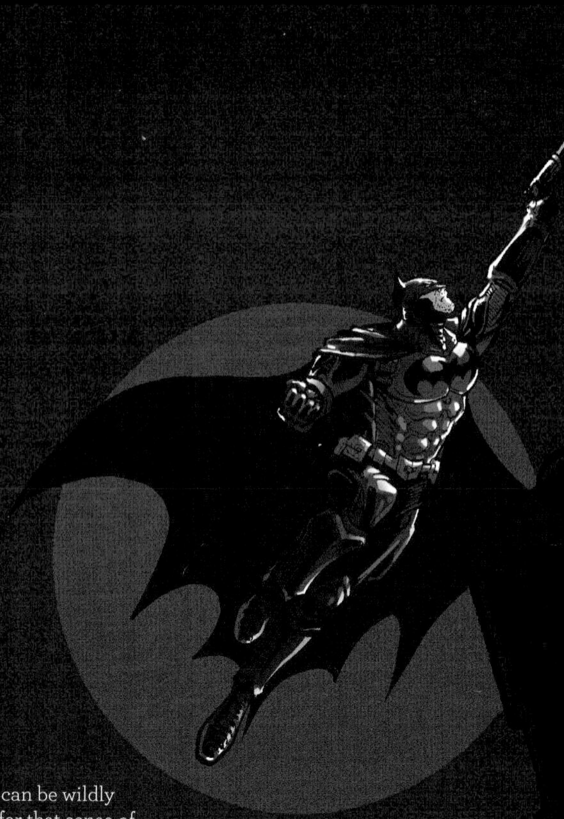

Floppy issues of comic books can be wildly entertaining, but they don't offer that sense of an active experience we get when we're online or in the middle of a game. Nowadays, there's a huge section of the audience that thinks stories about Batman are fun, but it'd be much more fun to *be* Batman and *live* the adventure.

So when DC Vice President for Integrated Publishing Hank Kanalz and Editor Jim Chadwick told me DC had partnered with Motion Books pioneer Madefire to produce a multipath digital graphic novel that would create that active experience, and asked if I wanted to be involved, I was all ears. What we'd be doing would be completely new to DC. We'd have to design the work process as we went along, and make changes to it in midstream. We'd have to teach ourselves this new kind of comics storytelling, and it would undoubtedly lead us to some dead ends, just as Batman would face in the story. And we'd need a team of innovative, energetic, forward-looking writers and artists (and me) to tell the story. In Doug Wagner, Frank Hannah, Christian Duce, Richard Ortiz, Federico Dallocchio, Vicente Cifuentes, Omar Francis, Victor Drujiniu and Thomas Derenick, DC found just the right people. I'm grateful to them, to Hank and Jim, to everyone at DC and Madefire for letting me be part of the groundbreaking. I'm so proud of what we did, and knowing that it will be a mold for future creators to develop or break as the medium moves into tomorrow is an incredible honor.

What is the future of comics?

Just turn the page (or swipe your finger).

Adam Beechen
Los Angeles, 2014

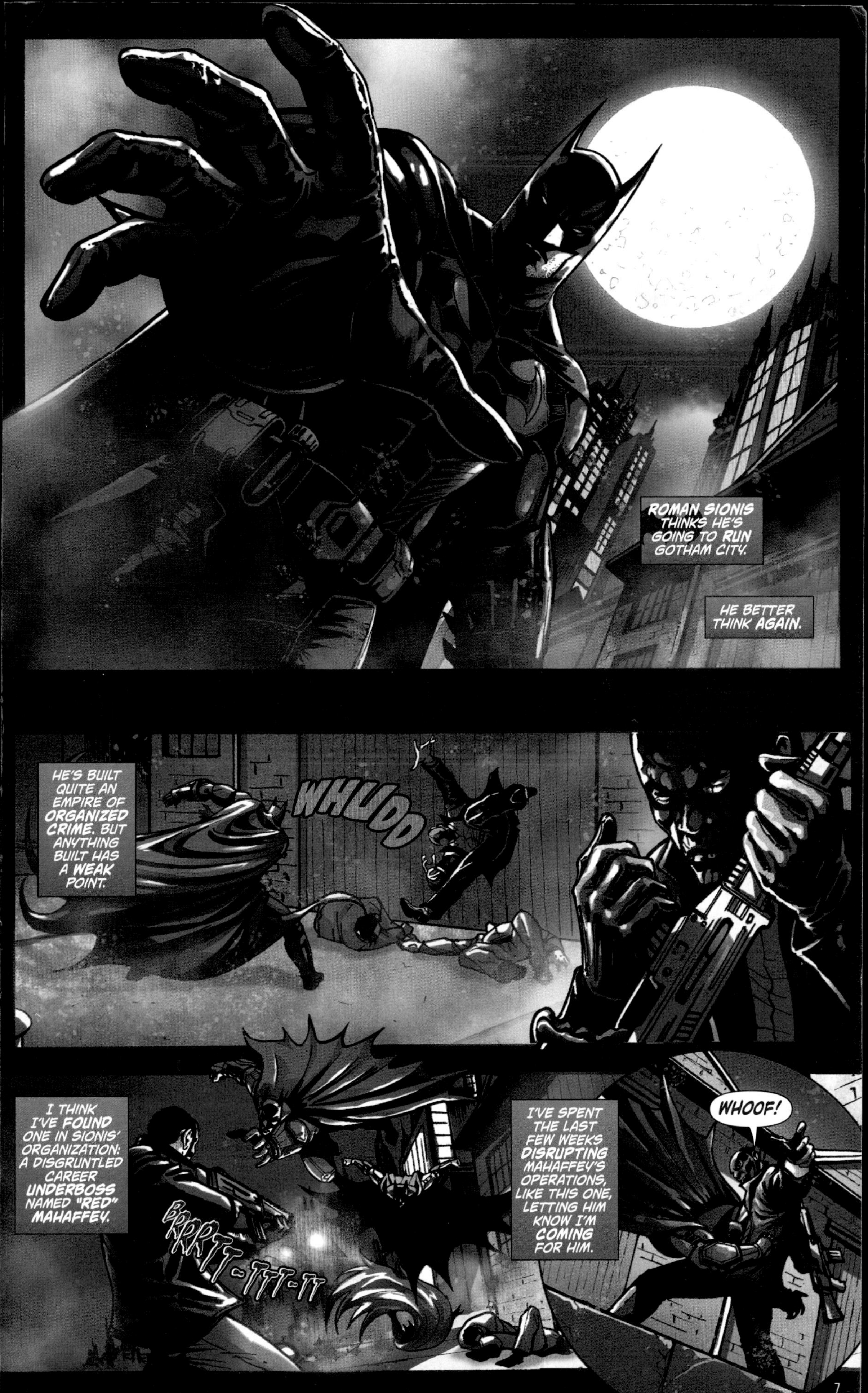
ROMAN SIONIS THINKS HE'S GOING TO RUN GOTHAM CITY.
HE BETTER THINK AGAIN.
HE'S BUILT QUITE AN EMPIRE OF ORGANIZED CRIME. BUT ANYTHING BUILT HAS A WEAK POINT.
WHUDD
I THINK I'VE FOUND ONE IN SIONIS' ORGANIZATION: A DISGRUNTLED CAREER UNDERBOSS NAMED "RED" MAHAFFEY.
BRRRTT-TTT-TT
I'VE SPENT THE LAST FEW WEEKS DISRUPTING MAHAFFEY'S OPERATIONS, LIKE THIS ONE, LETTING HIM KNOW I'M COMING FOR HIM.
WHOOF!

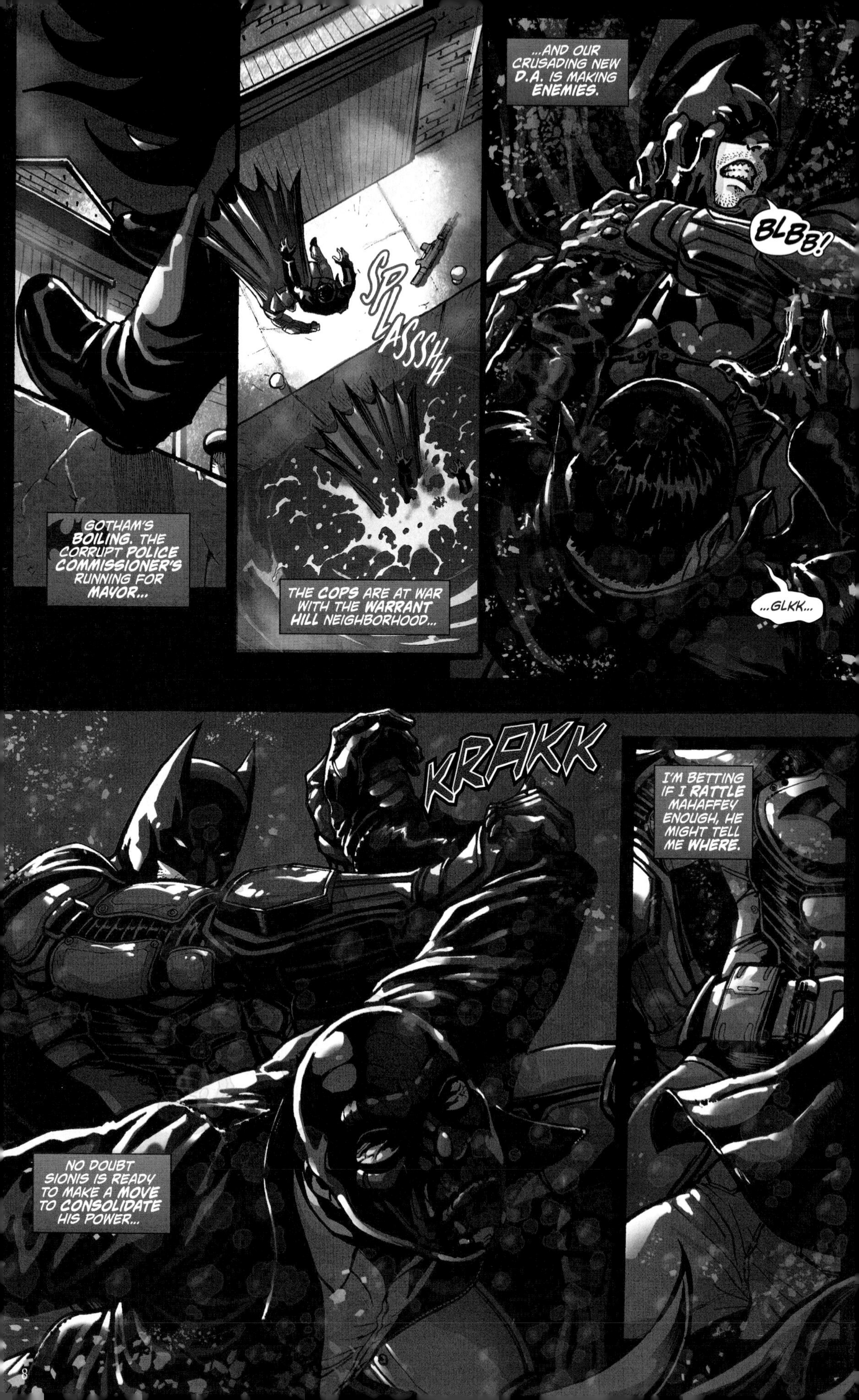
GOTHAM'S BOILING. THE CORRUPT POLICE COMMISSIONER'S RUNNING FOR MAYOR...
SPLASSSHH
THE COPS ARE AT WAR WITH THE WARRANT HILL NEIGHBORHOOD...
...AND OUR CRUSADING NEW D.A. IS MAKING ENEMIES.
BLBB!
...GLKK...
KRAKK
NO DOUBT SIONIS IS READY TO MAKE A MOVE TO CONSOLIDATE HIS POWER...
I'M BETTING IF I RATTLE MAHAFFEY ENOUGH, HE MIGHT TELL ME WHERE.

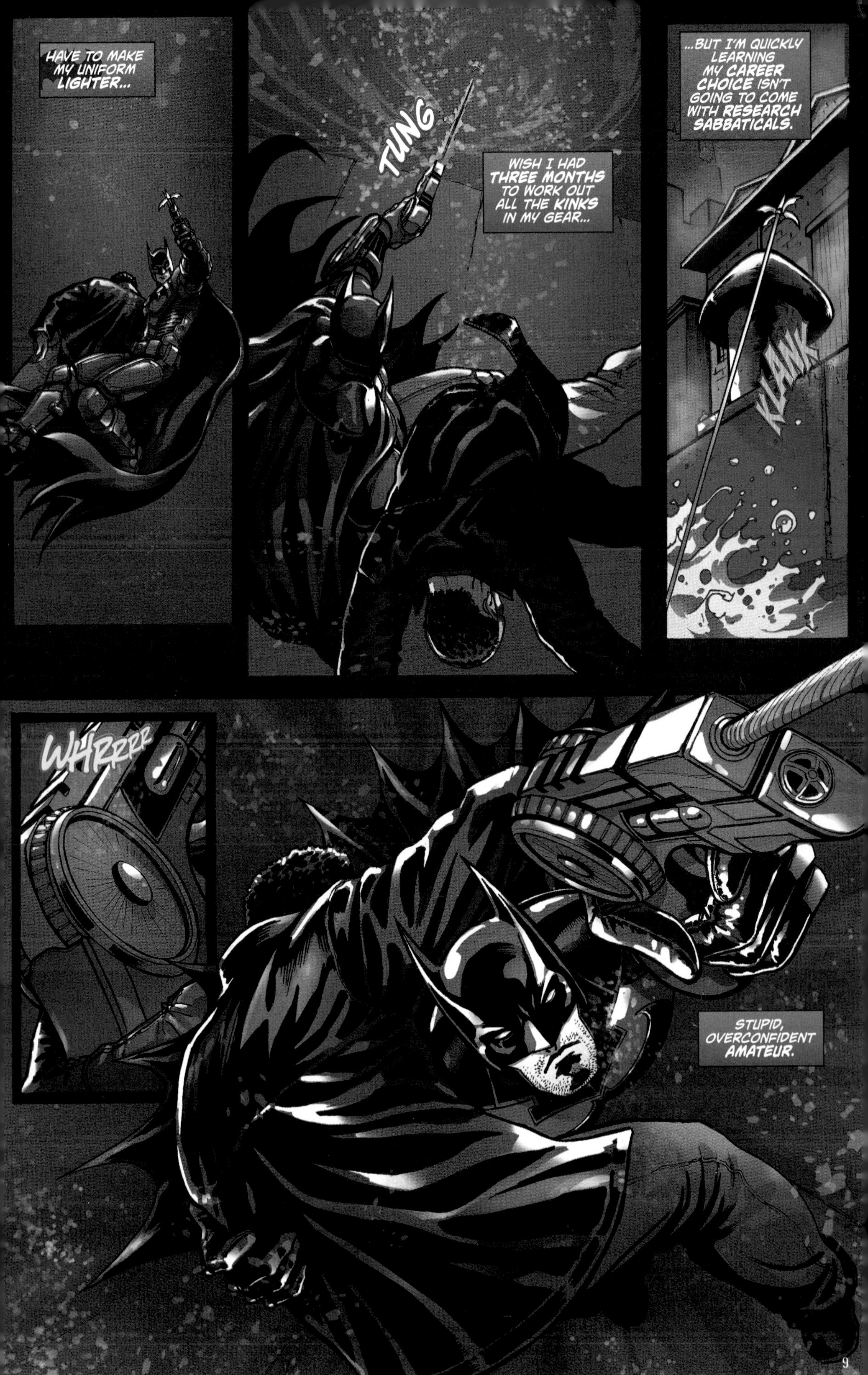
HAVE TO MAKE MY UNIFORM LIGHTER...
TUNG
WISH I HAD THREE MONTHS TO WORK OUT ALL THE KINKS IN MY GEAR...
...BUT I'M QUICKLY LEARNING MY CAREER CHOICE ISN'T GOING TO COME WITH RESEARCH SABBATICALS.
KLANK
WHRRRR
STUPID, OVERCONFIDENT AMATEUR.

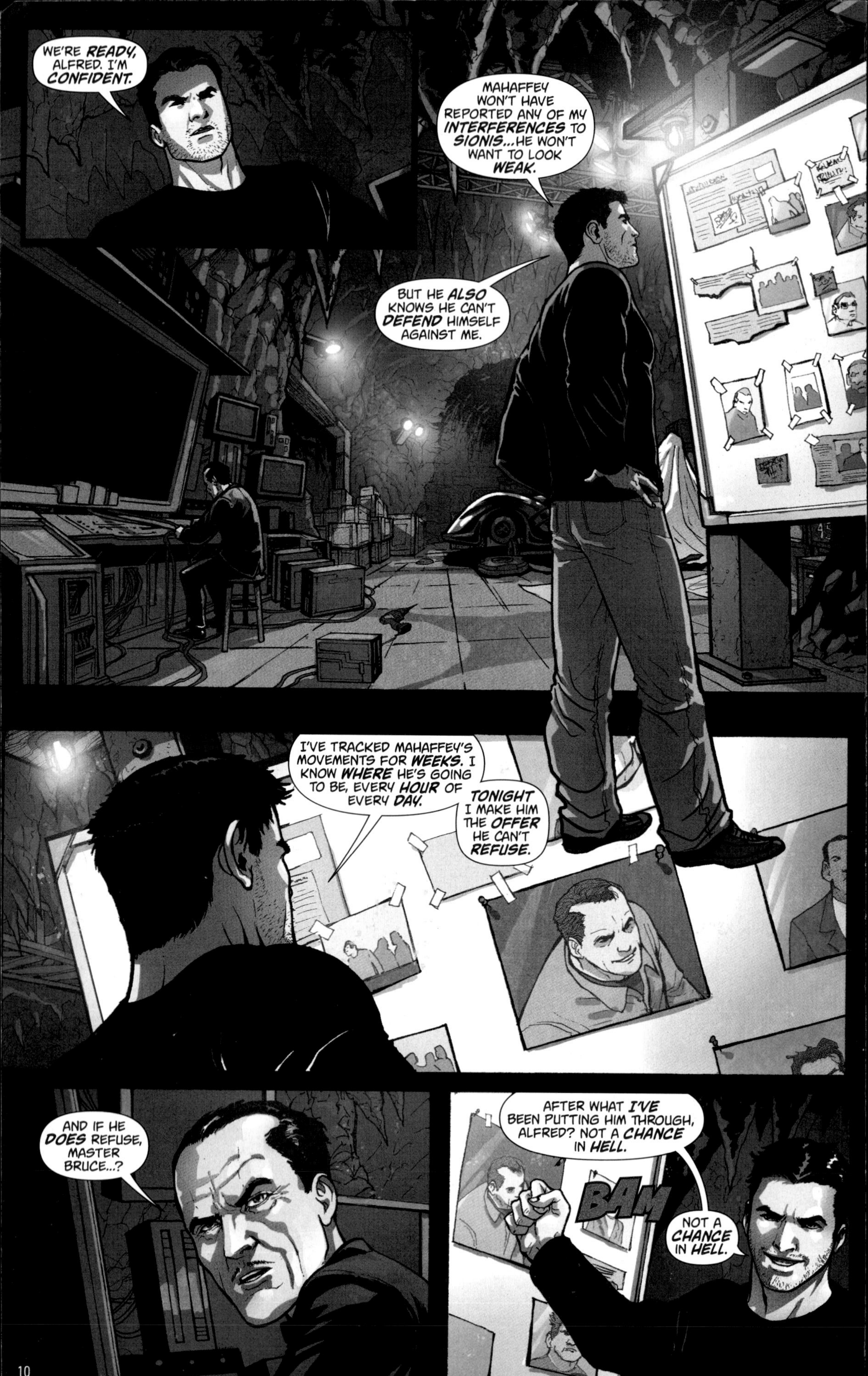
WE'RE READY, ALFRED. I'M CONFIDENT.
MAHAFFEY WON'T HAVE REPORTED ANY OF MY INTERFERENCES TO SIONIS...HE WON'T WANT TO LOOK WEAK.
BUT HE ALSO KNOWS HE CAN'T DEFEND HIMSELF AGAINST ME.
I'VE TRACKED MAHAFFEY'S MOVEMENTS FOR WEEKS. I KNOW WHERE HE'S GOING TO BE, EVERY HOUR OF EVERY DAY.
TONIGHT I MAKE HIM THE OFFER HE CAN'T REFUSE.
AND IF HE DOES REFUSE, MASTER BRUCE...?
AFTER WHAT I'VE BEEN PUTTING HIM THROUGH, ALFRED? NOT A CHANCE IN HELL.
BAM
NOT A CHANCE IN HELL.

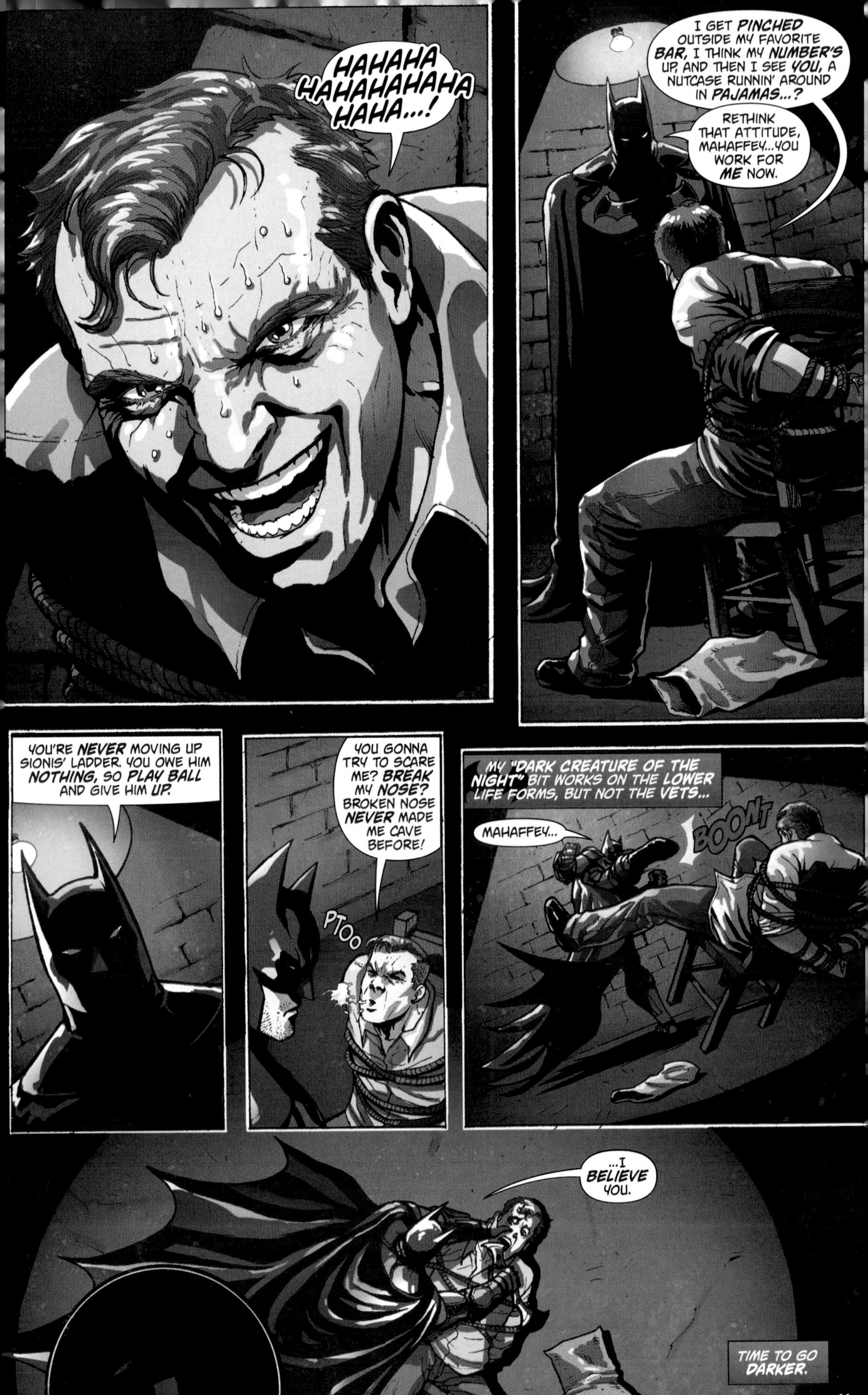
HAHAHA HAHAHAHAHA HAHA...!
I GET PINCHED OUTSIDE MY FAVORITE BAR, I THINK MY NUMBER'S UP, AND THEN I SEE YOU, A NUTCASE RUNNIN' AROUND IN PAJAMAS...?
RETHINK THAT ATTITUDE, MAHAFFEY...YOU WORK FOR ME NOW.
YOU'RE NEVER MOVING UP SIONIS' LADDER. YOU OWE HIM NOTHING, SO PLAY BALL AND GIVE HIM UP.
YOU GONNA TRY TO SCARE ME? BREAK MY NOSE? BROKEN NOSE NEVER MADE ME CAVE BEFORE!
PTOO
MY "DARK CREATURE OF THE NIGHT" BIT WORKS ON THE LOWER LIFE FORMS, BUT NOT THE VETS...
MAHAFFEY...
BOONT
...I BELIEVE YOU.
TIME TO GO DARKER.

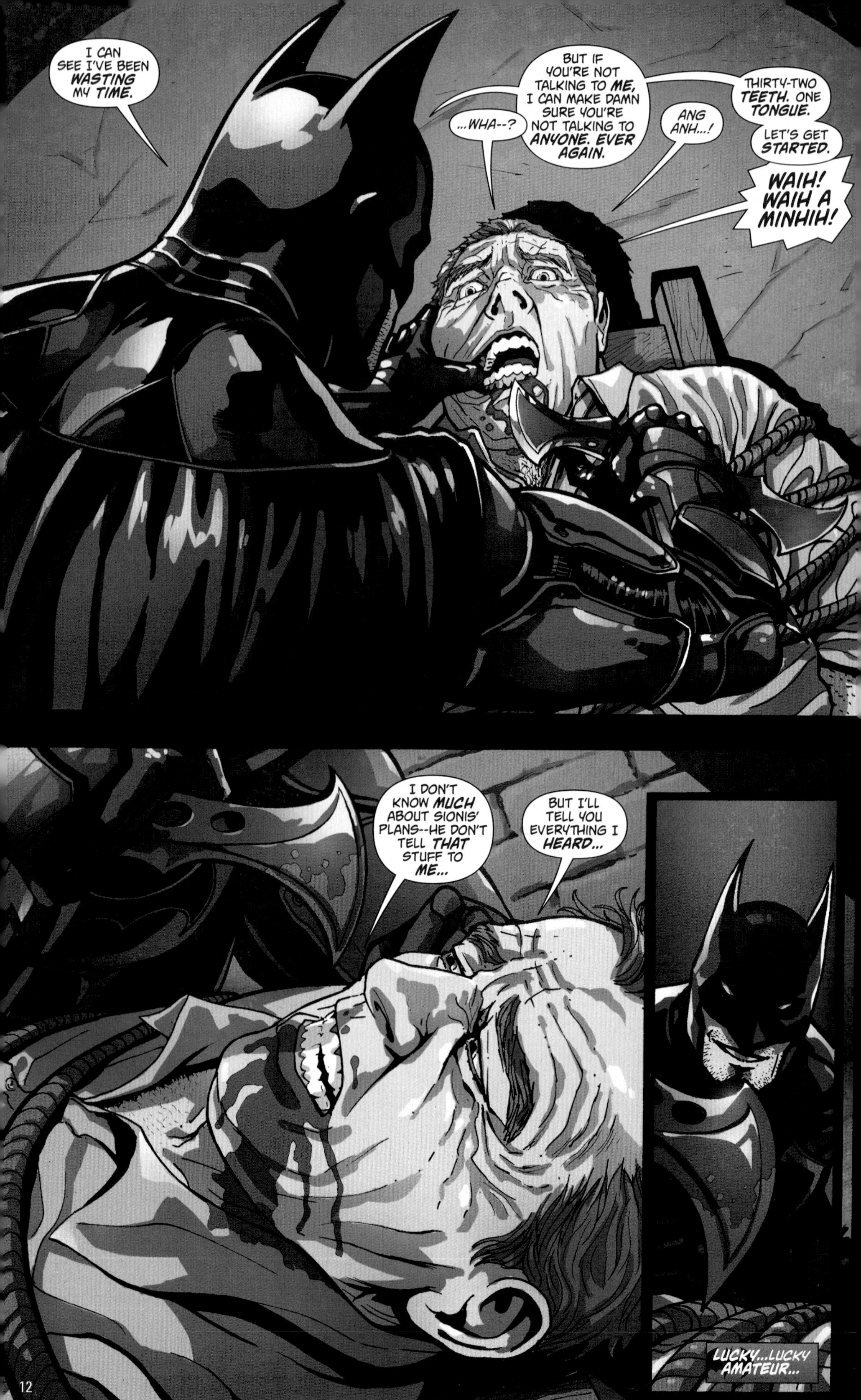
I CAN SEE I'VE BEEN WASTING MY TIME.
...WHA--?
BUT IF YOU'RE NOT TALKING TO ME, I CAN MAKE DAMN SURE YOU'RE NOT TALKING TO ANYONE. EVER AGAIN.
ANG ANH...!
THIRTY-TWO TEETH. ONE TONGUE.
LET'S GET STARTED.
WAIH! WAIH A MINHIH!
I DON'T KNOW MUCH ABOUT SIONIS' PLANS--HE DON'T TELL THAT STUFF TO ME...
BUT I'LL TELL YOU EVERYTHING I HEARD...
LUCKY...LUCKY AMATEUR...

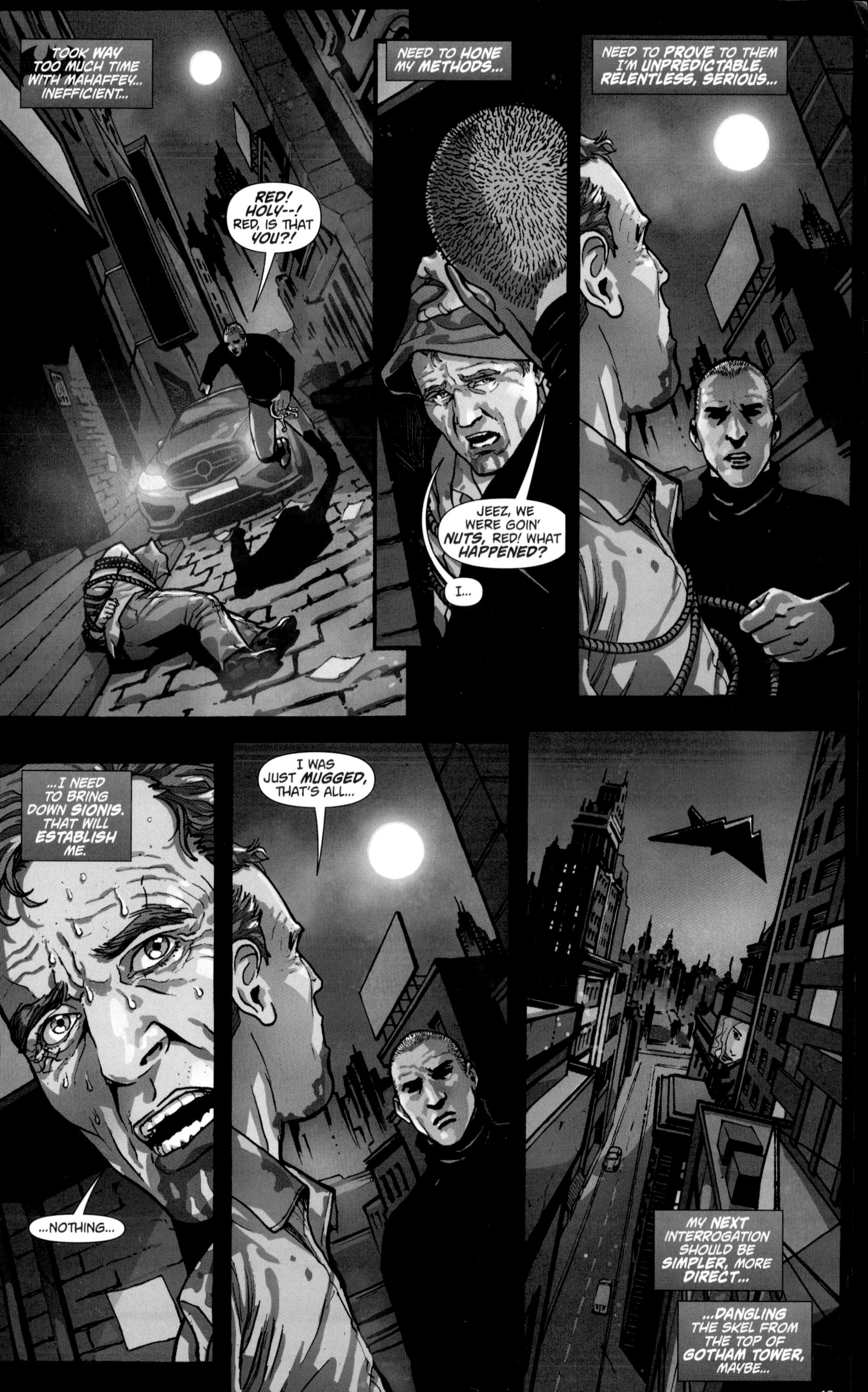
TOOK WAY TOO MUCH TIME WITH MAHAFFEY... INEFFICIENT...
RED! HOLY--! RED, IS THAT YOU?!
NEED TO HONE MY METHODS...
JEEZ, WE WERE GOIN' NUTS, RED! WHAT HAPPENED?
I...
NEED TO PROVE TO THEM I'M UNPREDICTABLE, RELENTLESS, SERIOUS...
...I NEED TO BRING DOWN SIONIS. THAT WILL ESTABLISH ME.
...NOTHING...
I WAS JUST MUGGED, THAT'S ALL...
MY NEXT INTERROGATION SHOULD BE SIMPLER, MORE DIRECT...
...DANGLING THE SKEL FROM THE TOP OF GOTHAM TOWER, MAYBE...

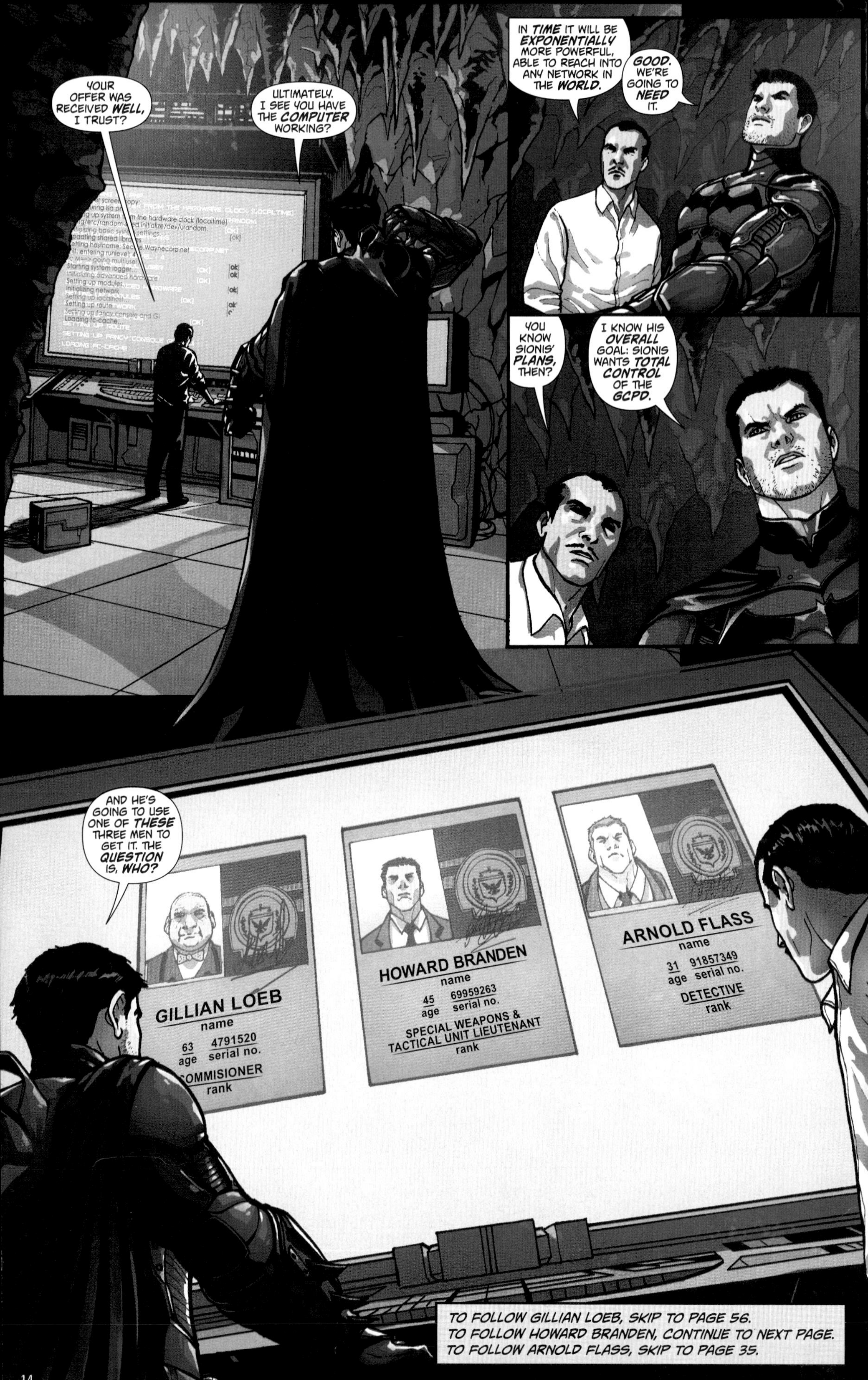
YOUR OFFER WAS RECEIVED WELL, I TRUST?
ULTIMATELY. I SEE YOU HAVE THE COMPUTER WORKING?
IN TIME IT WILL BE EXPONENTIALLY MORE POWERFUL, ABLE TO REACH INTO ANY NETWORK IN THE WORLD.
GOOD. WE'RE GOING TO NEED IT.
YOU KNOW SIONIS' PLANS, THEN?
I KNOW HIS OVERALL GOAL: SIONIS WANTS TOTAL CONTROL OF THE GCPD.
AND HE'S GOING TO USE ONE OF THESE THREE MEN TO GET IT. THE QUESTION IS, WHO?
GILLIAN LOEB
name
63 age
4791520 serial no.
COMMISIONER
rank
HOWARD BRANDEN
name
45 age
69959263 serial no.
SPECIAL WEAPONS & TACTICAL UNIT LIEUTENANT
rank
ARNOLD FLASS
name
31 age
91857349 serial no.
DETECTIVE
rank
TO FOLLOW GILLIAN LOEB, SKIP TO PAGE 56.
TO FOLLOW HOWARD BRANDEN, CONTINUE TO NEXT PAGE.
TO FOLLOW ARNOLD FLASS, SKIP TO PAGE 35.

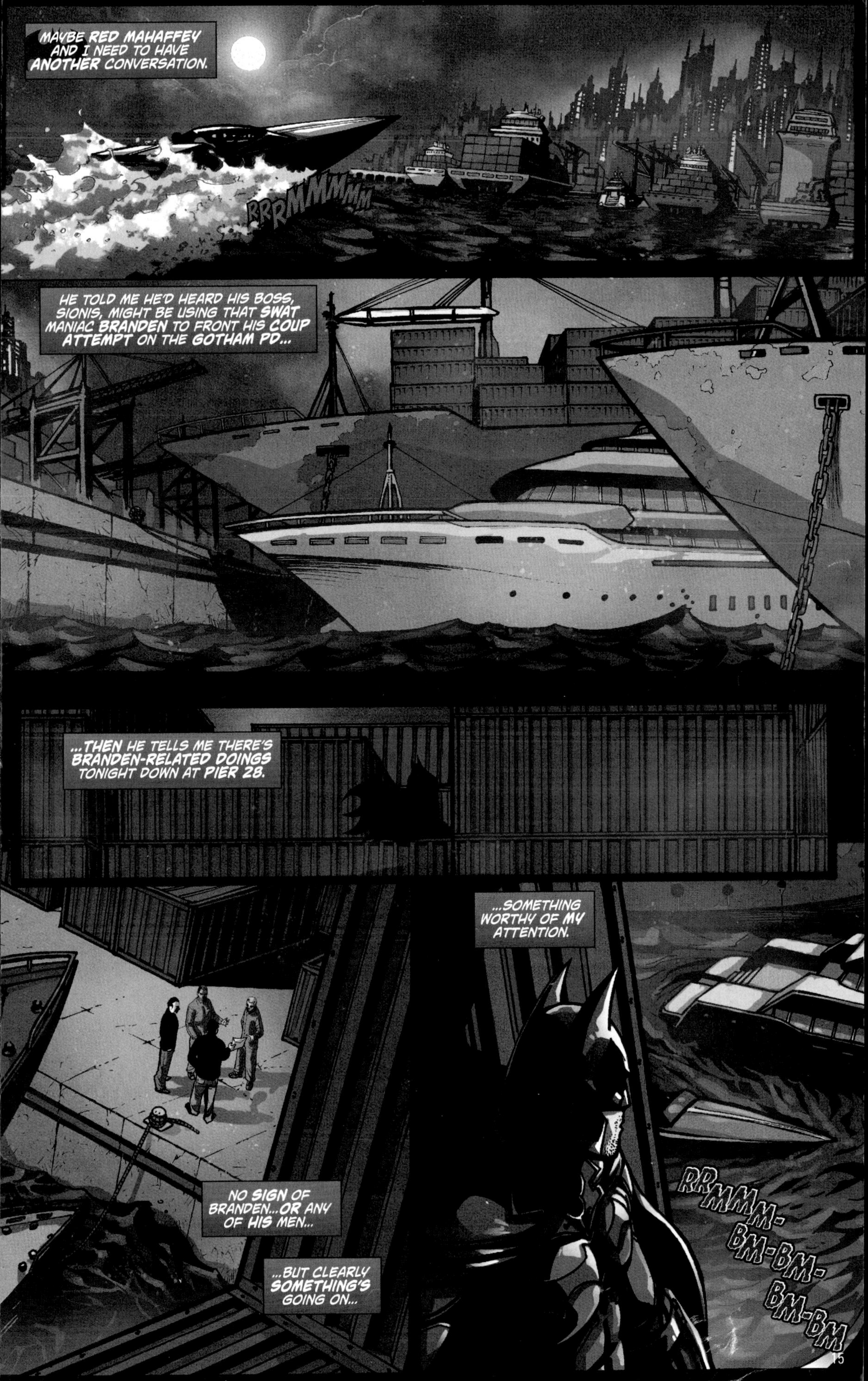
MAYBE RED MAHAFFEY AND I NEED TO HAVE ANOTHER CONVERSATION.
RRRMMMMMM
HE TOLD ME HE'D HEARD HIS BOSS, SIONIS, MIGHT BE USING THAT SWAT MANIAC BRANDEN TO FRONT HIS COUP ATTEMPT ON THE GOTHAM PD...
...THEN HE TELLS ME THERE'S BRANDEN-RELATED DOINGS TONIGHT DOWN AT PIER 28.
...SOMETHING WORTHY OF MY ATTENTION.
NO SIGN OF BRANDEN...OR ANY OF HIS MEN...
...BUT CLEARLY SOMETHING'S GOING ON...
RRMMMM-BM-BM-BM-BM

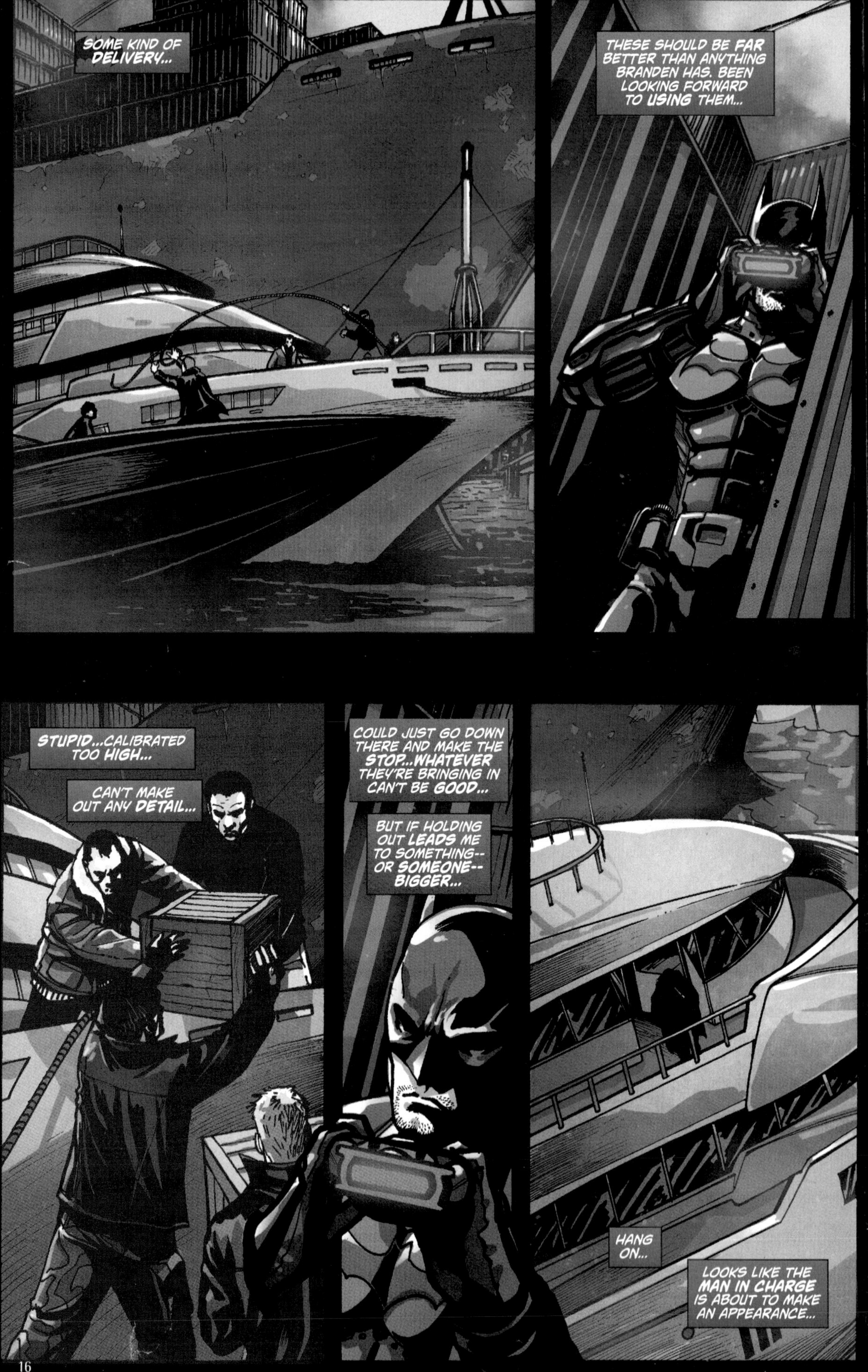
SOME KIND OF DELIVERY...
THESE SHOULD BE FAR BETTER THAN ANYTHING BRANDEN HAS. BEEN LOOKING FORWARD TO USING THEM...
STUPID...CALIBRATED TOO HIGH...
CAN'T MAKE OUT ANY DETAIL...
COULD JUST GO DOWN THERE AND MAKE THE STOP...WHATEVER THEY'RE BRINGING IN CAN'T BE GOOD...
BUT IF HOLDING OUT LEADS ME TO SOMETHING-- OR SOMEONE-- BIGGER...
HANG ON...
LOOKS LIKE THE MAN IN CHARGE IS ABOUT TO MAKE AN APPEARANCE...

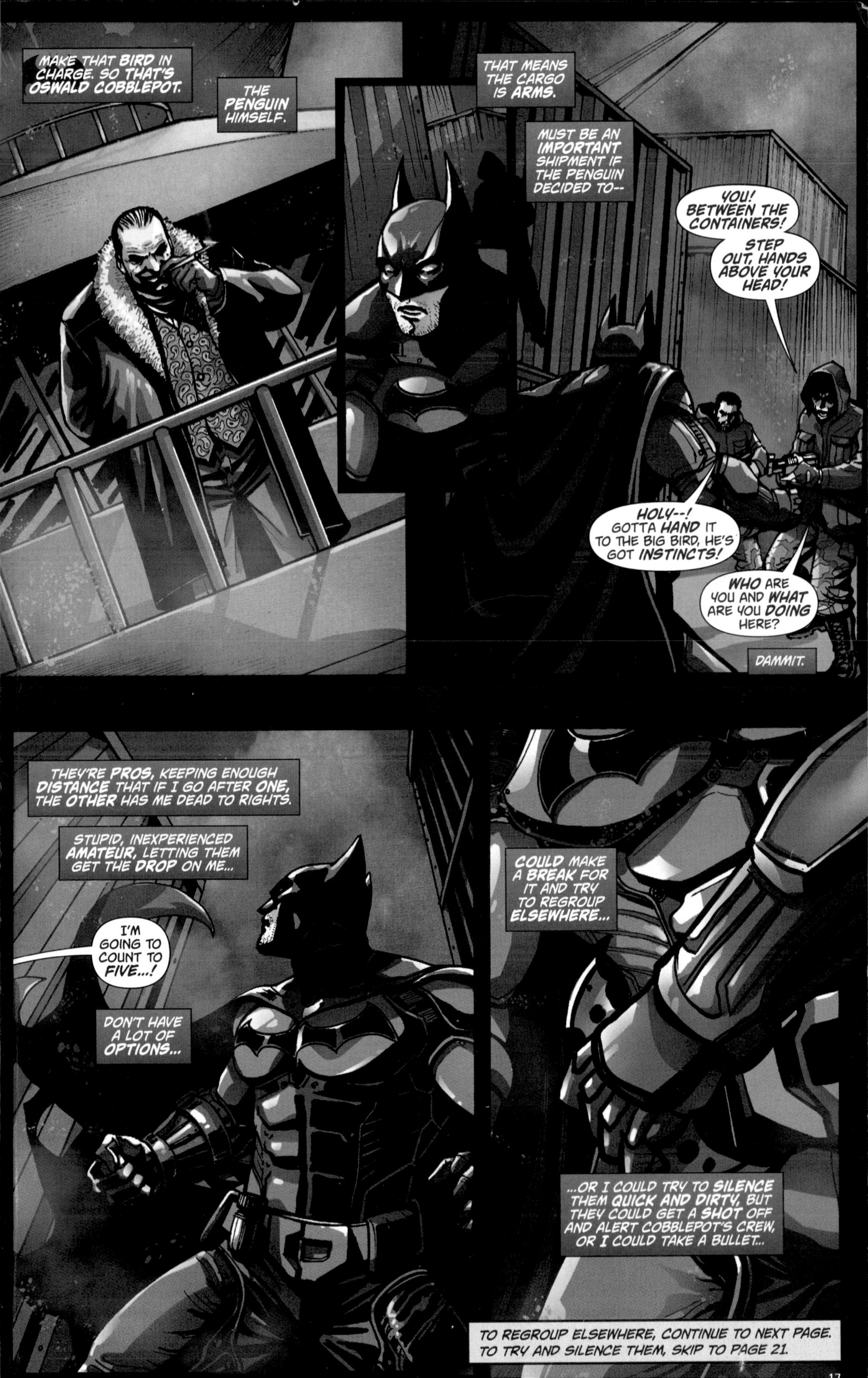
MAKE THAT BIRD IN CHARGE. SO THAT'S OSWALD COBBLEPOT.
THE PENGUIN HIMSELF.
THAT MEANS THE CARGO IS ARMS.
MUST BE AN IMPORTANT SHIPMENT IF THE PENGUIN DECIDED TO--
YOU! BETWEEN THE CONTAINERS!
STEP OUT, HANDS ABOVE YOUR HEAD!
HOLY--! GOTTA HAND IT TO THE BIG BIRD, HE'S GOT INSTINCTS!
WHO ARE YOU AND WHAT ARE YOU DOING HERE?
DAMMIT.
THEY'RE PROS, KEEPING ENOUGH DISTANCE THAT IF I GO AFTER ONE, THE OTHER HAS ME DEAD TO RIGHTS.
STUPID, INEXPERIENCED AMATEUR, LETTING THEM GET THE DROP ON ME...
I'M GOING TO COUNT TO FIVE...!
DON'T HAVE A LOT OF OPTIONS...
COULD MAKE A BREAK FOR IT AND TRY TO REGROUP ELSEWHERE...
...OR I COULD TRY TO SILENCE THEM QUICK AND DIRTY, BUT THEY COULD GET A SHOT OFF AND ALERT COBBLEPOT'S CREW, OR I COULD TAKE A BULLET...
TO REGROUP ELSEWHERE, CONTINUE TO NEXT PAGE.
TO TRY AND SILENCE THEM, SKIP TO PAGE 21.

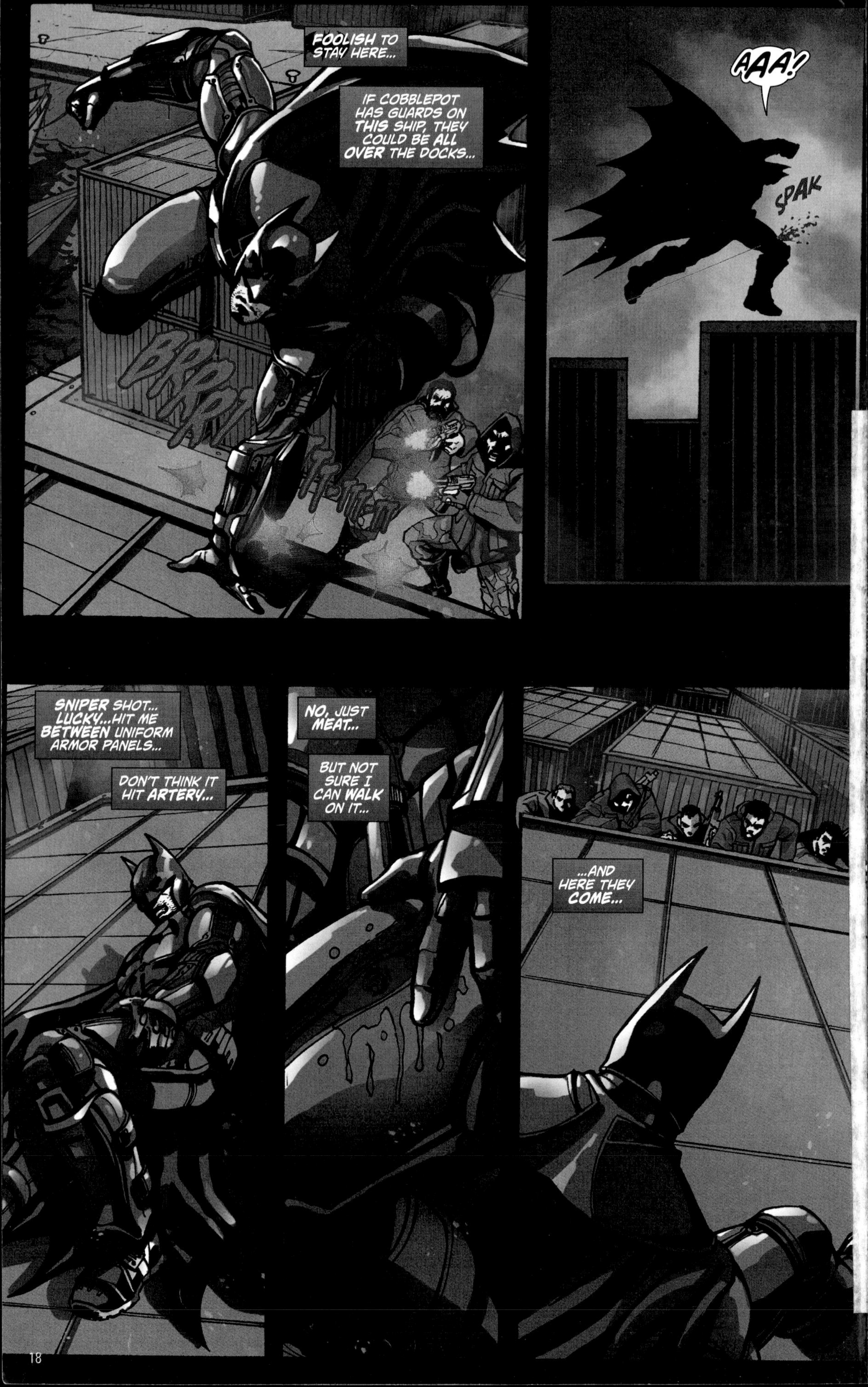
FOOLISH TO STAY HERE...
IF COBBLEPOT HAS GUARDS ON THIS SHIP, THEY COULD BE ALL OVER THE DOCKS...
AAA!
SPAK
SNIPER SHOT... LUCKY...HIT ME BETWEEN UNIFORM ARMOR PANELS...
DON'T THINK IT HIT ARTERY...
NO, JUST MEAT...
BUT NOT SURE I CAN WALK ON IT...
...AND HERE THEY COME...

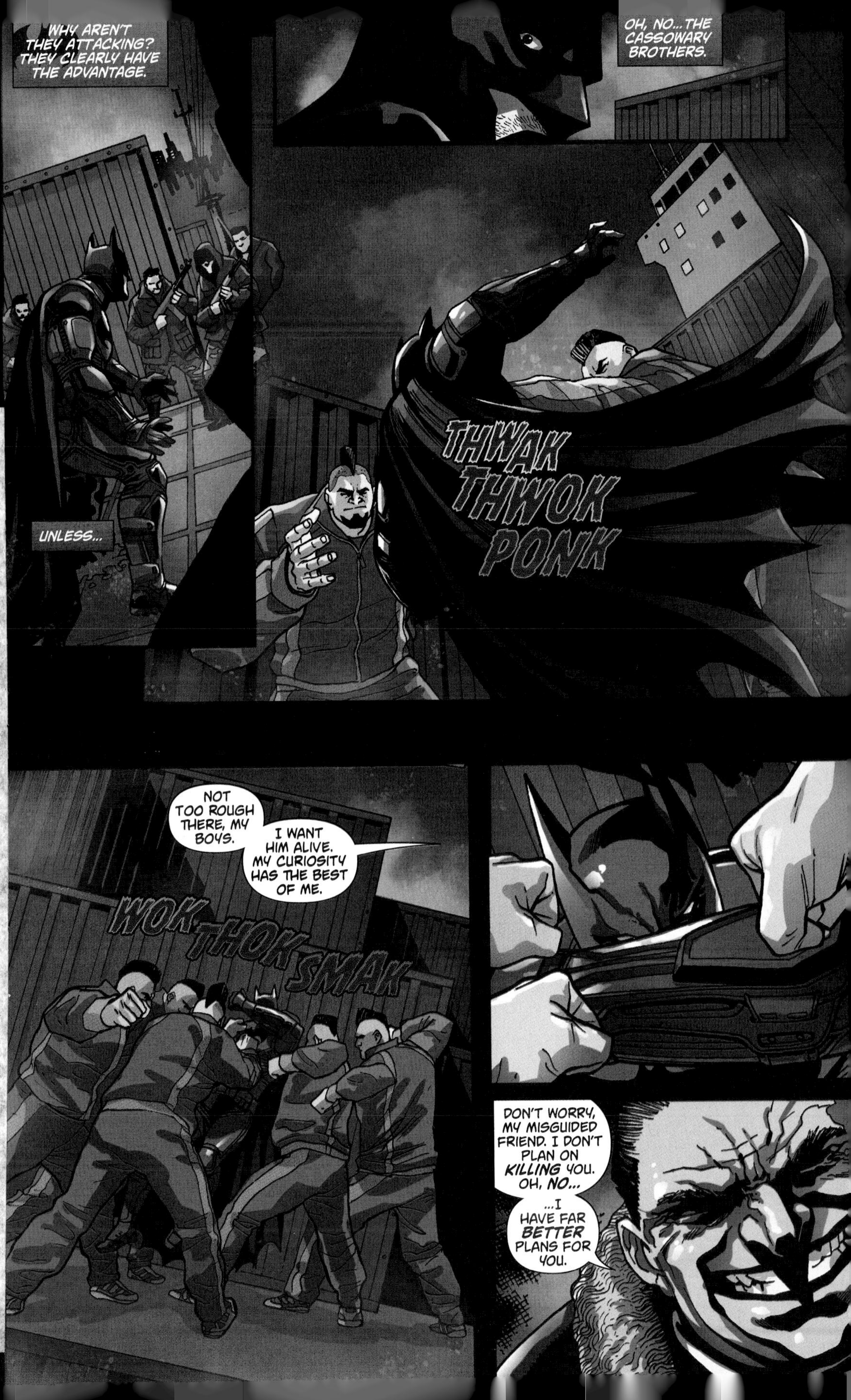
WHY AREN'T THEY ATTACKING? THEY CLEARLY HAVE THE ADVANTAGE.
UNLESS...
OH, NO...THE CASSOWARY BROTHERS.
THWAK
THWOK
PONK
NOT TOO ROUGH THERE, MY BOYS.
I WANT HIM ALIVE. MY CURIOSITY HAS THE BEST OF ME.
WOK
THOK
SMAK
DON'T WORRY, MY MISGUIDED FRIEND. I DON'T PLAN ON *KILLING* YOU. OH, *NO...*
...I HAVE FAR *BETTER* PLANS FOR YOU.

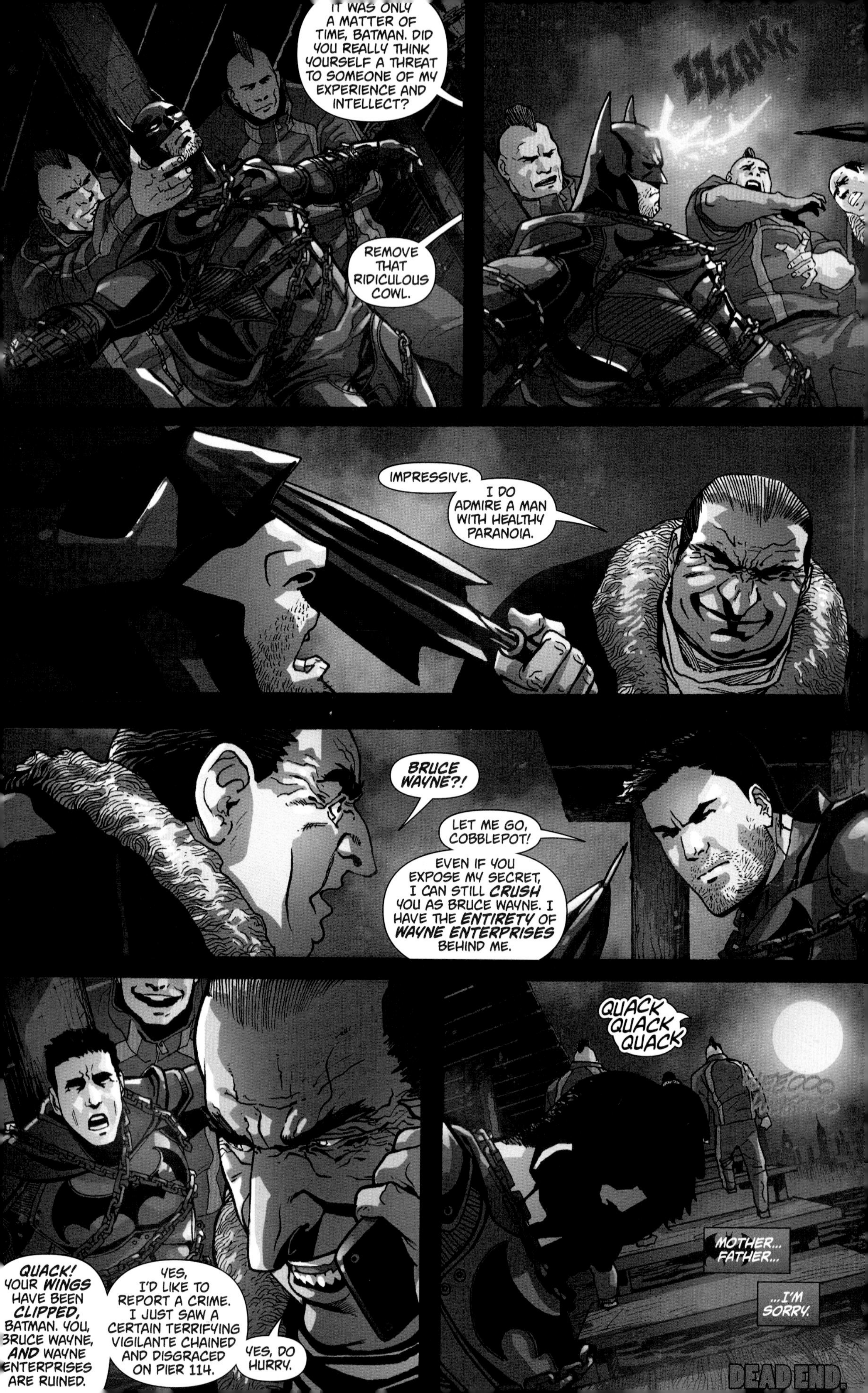
IT WAS ONLY A MATTER OF TIME, BATMAN. DID YOU REALLY THINK YOURSELF A THREAT TO SOMEONE OF MY EXPERIENCE AND INTELLECT?
REMOVE THAT RIDICULOUS COWL.
ZZZZAKK
IMPRESSIVE.
I DO ADMIRE A MAN WITH HEALTHY PARANOIA.
BRUCE WAYNE?!
LET ME GO, COBBLEPOT!
EVEN IF YOU EXPOSE MY SECRET, I CAN STILL CRUSH YOU AS BRUCE WAYNE. I HAVE THE ENTIRETY OF WAYNE ENTERPRISES BEHIND ME.
QUACK! YOUR WINGS HAVE BEEN CLIPPED, BATMAN. YOU, BRUCE WAYNE, AND WAYNE ENTERPRISES ARE RUINED.
YES, I'D LIKE TO REPORT A CRIME. I JUST SAW A CERTAIN TERRIFYING VIGILANTE CHAINED AND DISGRACED ON PIER 114.
YES, DO HURRY.
QUACK QUACK QUACK
MOTHER... FATHER...
...I'M SORRY.
DEAD END.

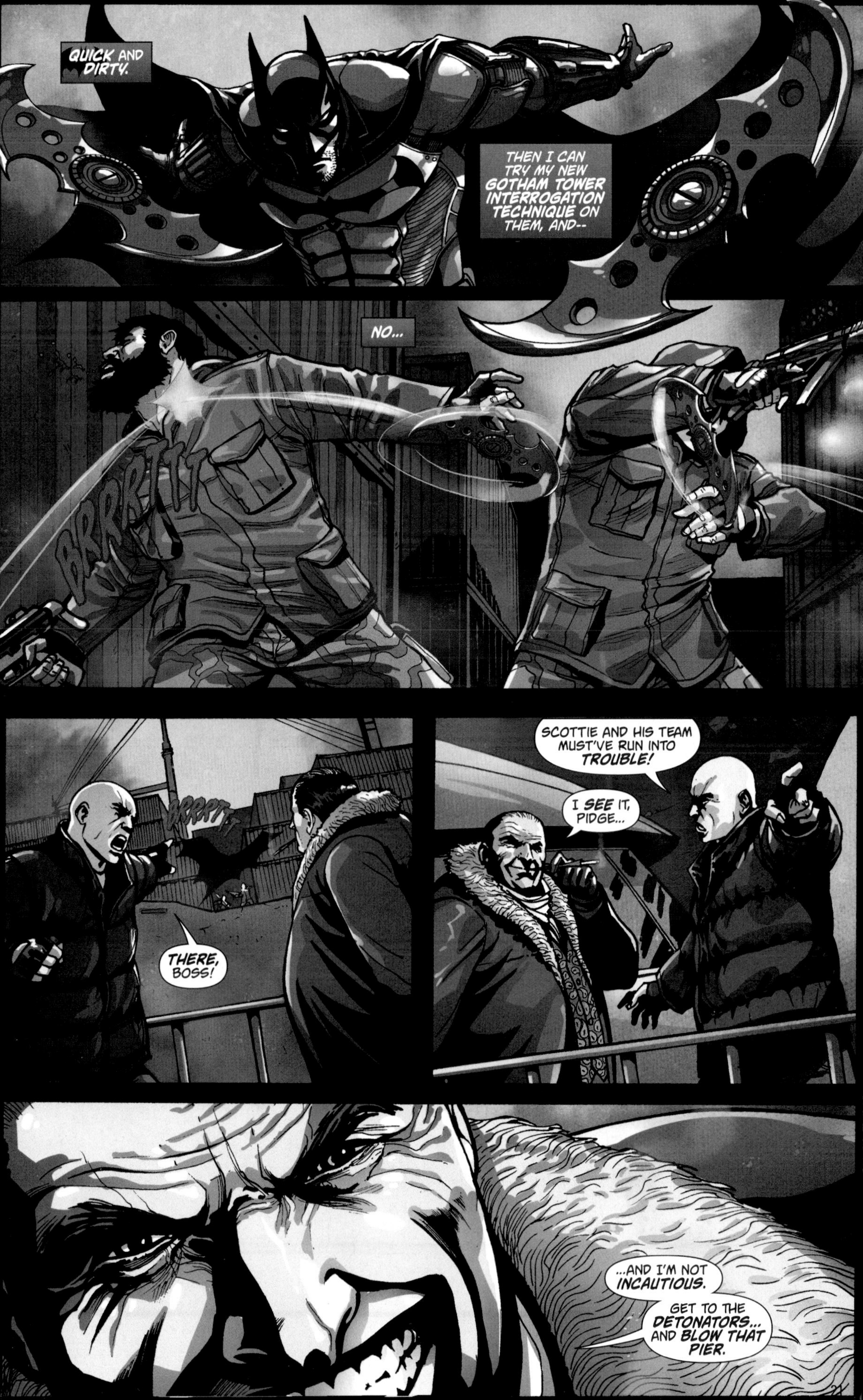
QUICK AND DIRTY.
THEN I CAN TRY MY NEW GOTHAM TOWER INTERROGATION TECHNIQUE ON THEM, AND--
NO...
BRRRTTT
BRRRTTT
THERE, BOSS!
SCOTTIE AND HIS TEAM MUST'VE RUN INTO TROUBLE!
I SEE IT, PIDGE...
...AND I'M NOT INCAUTIOUS.
GET TO THE DETONATORS... AND BLOW THAT PIER.

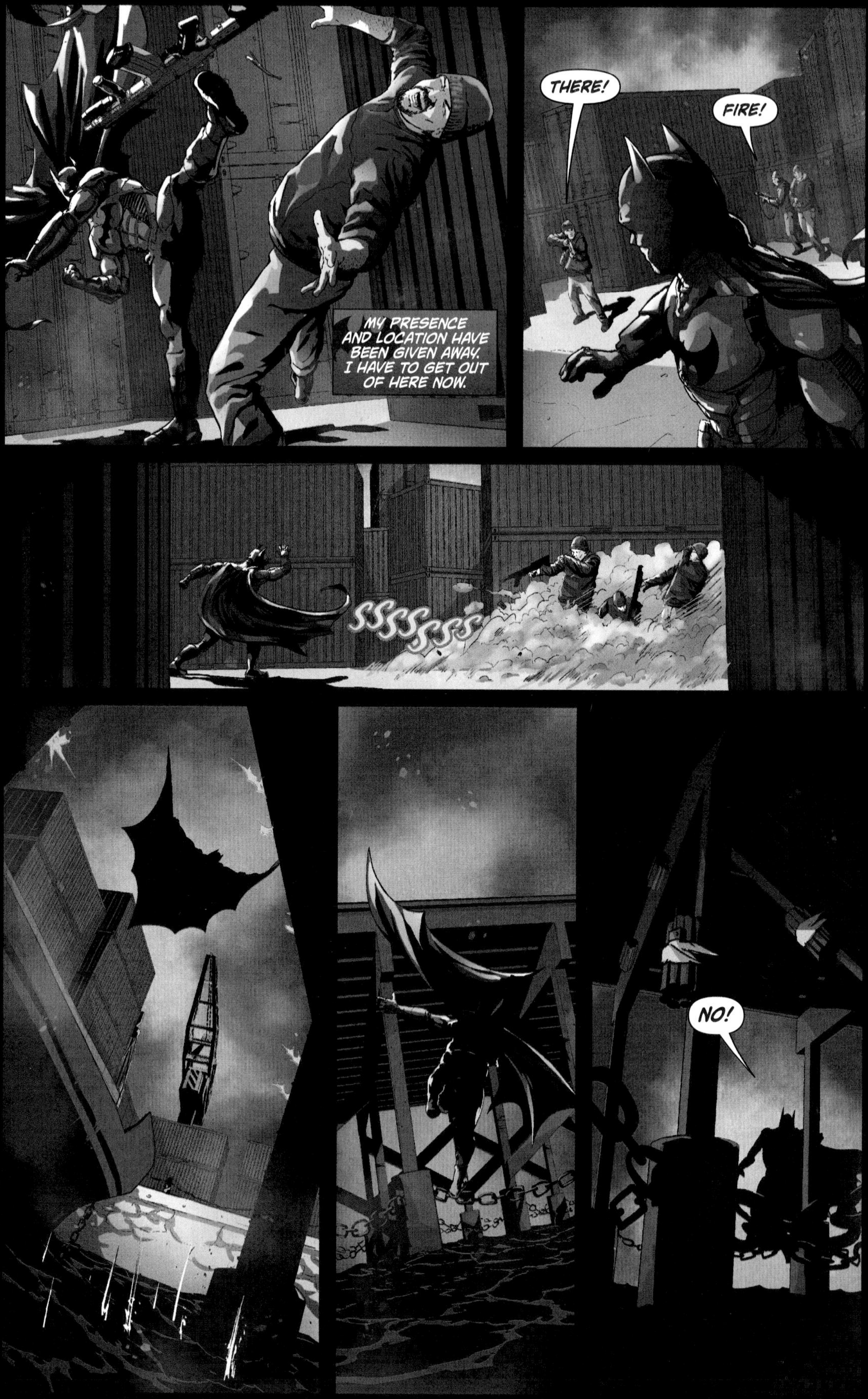
MY PRESENCE AND LOCATION HAVE BEEN GIVEN AWAY. I HAVE TO GET OUT OF HERE NOW.
THERE!
FIRE!
SSSSSSS
NO!

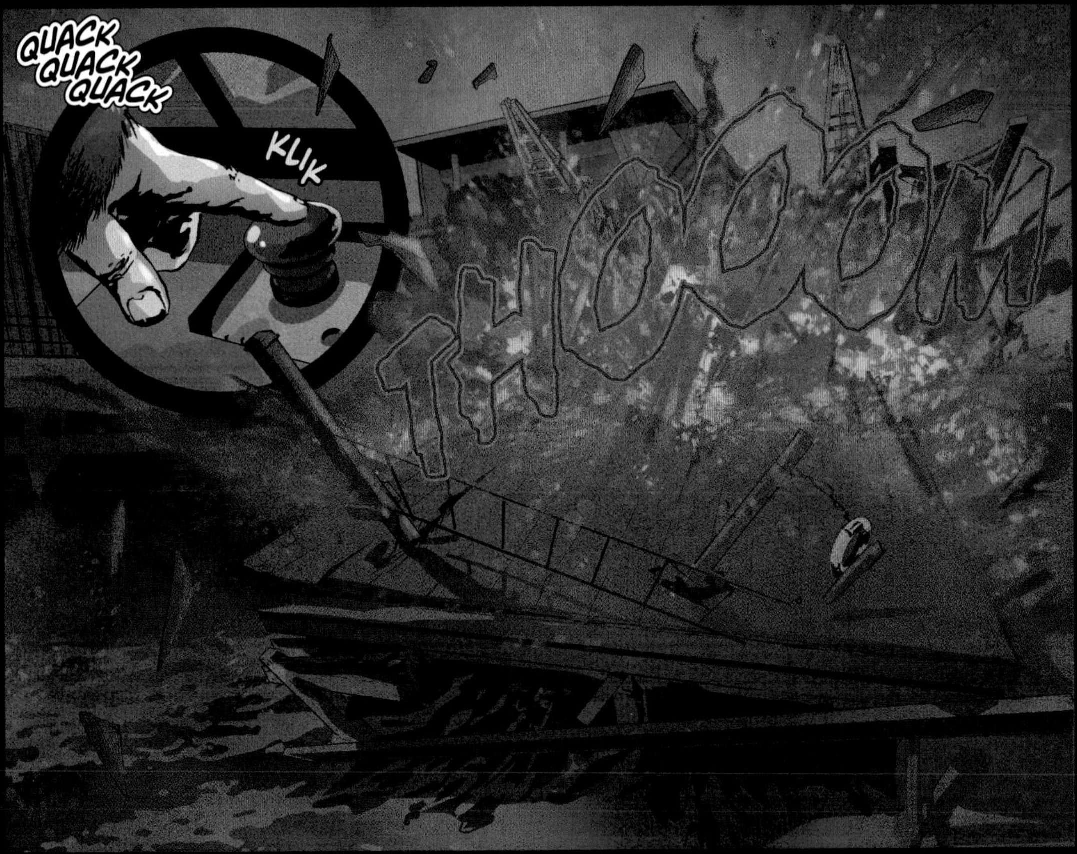
QUACK QUACK QUACK
KLIK
THOOOOOM

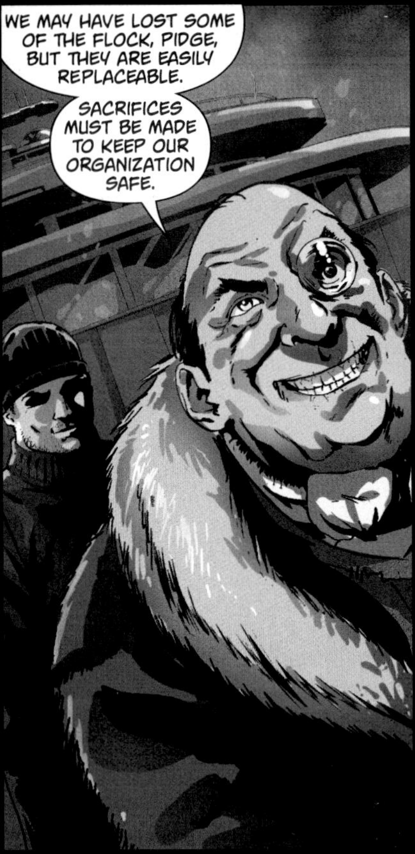
WE MAY HAVE LOST SOME OF THE FLOCK, PIDGE, BUT THEY ARE EASILY REPLACEABLE.
SACRIFICES MUST BE MADE TO KEEP OUR ORGANIZATION SAFE.

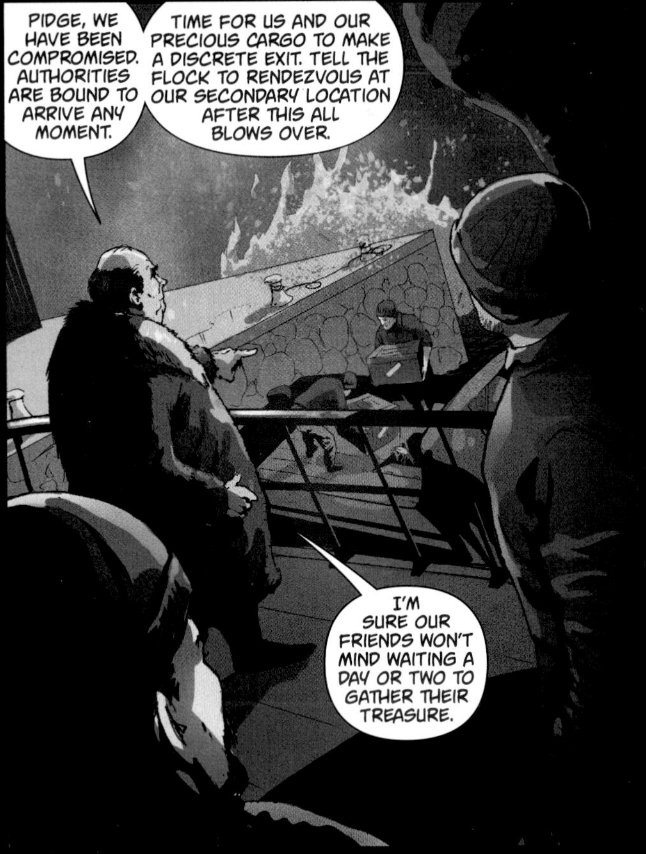
PIDGE, WE HAVE BEEN COMPROMISED. AUTHORITIES ARE BOUND TO ARRIVE ANY MOMENT.
TIME FOR US AND OUR PRECIOUS CARGO TO MAKE A DISCRETE EXIT. TELL THE FLOCK TO RENDEZVOUS AT OUR SECONDARY LOCATION AFTER THIS ALL BLOWS OVER.
I'M SURE OUR FRIENDS WON'T MIND WAITING A DAY OR TWO TO GATHER THEIR TREASURE.

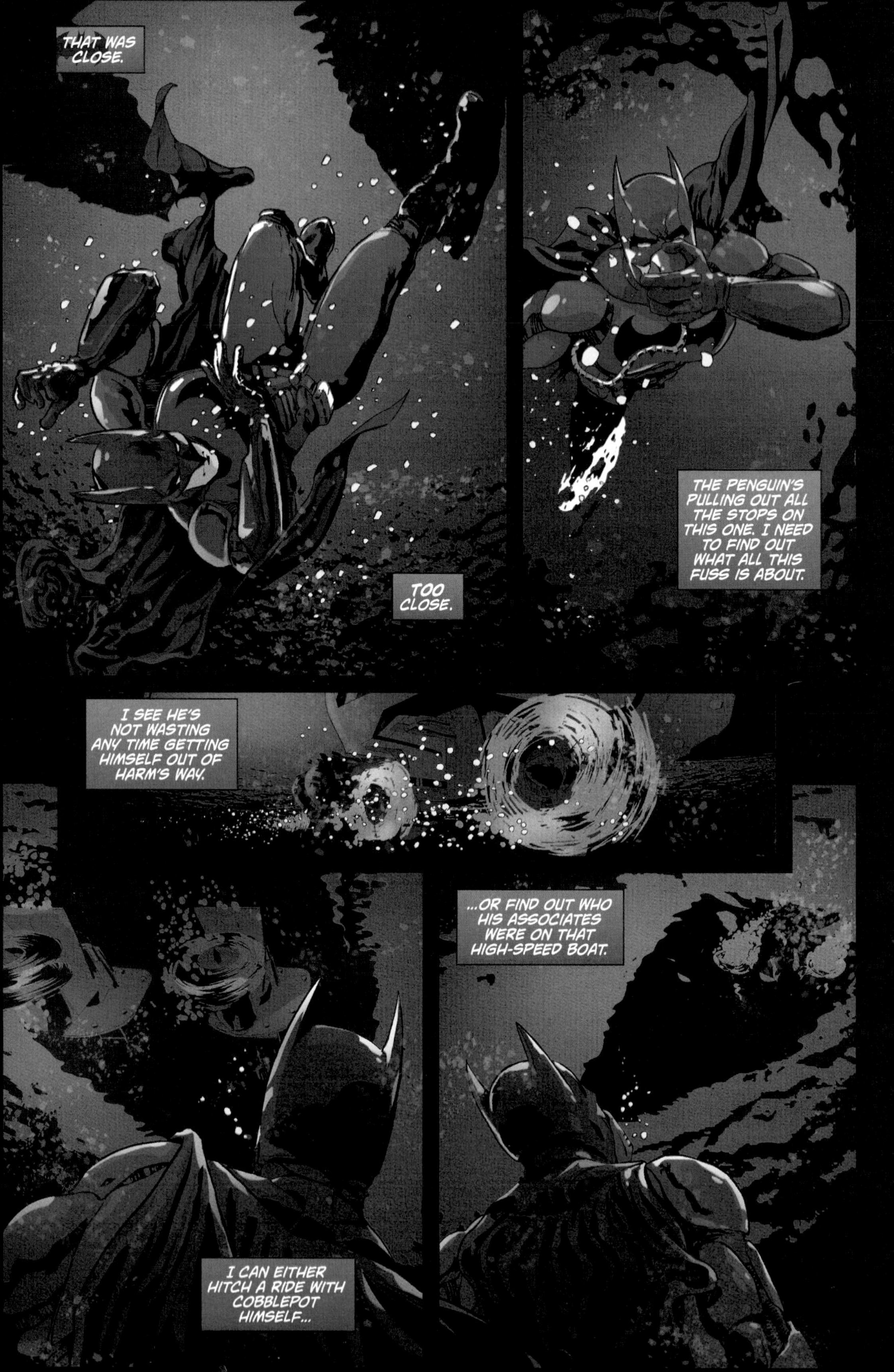
THAT WAS CLOSE.
TOO CLOSE.
THE PENGUIN'S PULLING OUT ALL THE STOPS ON THIS ONE. I NEED TO FIND OUT WHAT ALL THIS FUSS IS ABOUT.
I SEE HE'S NOT WASTING ANY TIME GETTING HIMSELF OUT OF HARM'S WAY.
I CAN EITHER HITCH A RIDE WITH COBBLEPOT HIMSELF...
...OR FIND OUT WHO HIS ASSOCIATES WERE ON THAT HIGH-SPEED BOAT.

TO FOLLOW COBBLEPOT, CONTINUE TO NEXT PAGE.
TO FIND OUT WHO HE'S WORKING WITH, SKIP TO PAGE 32.

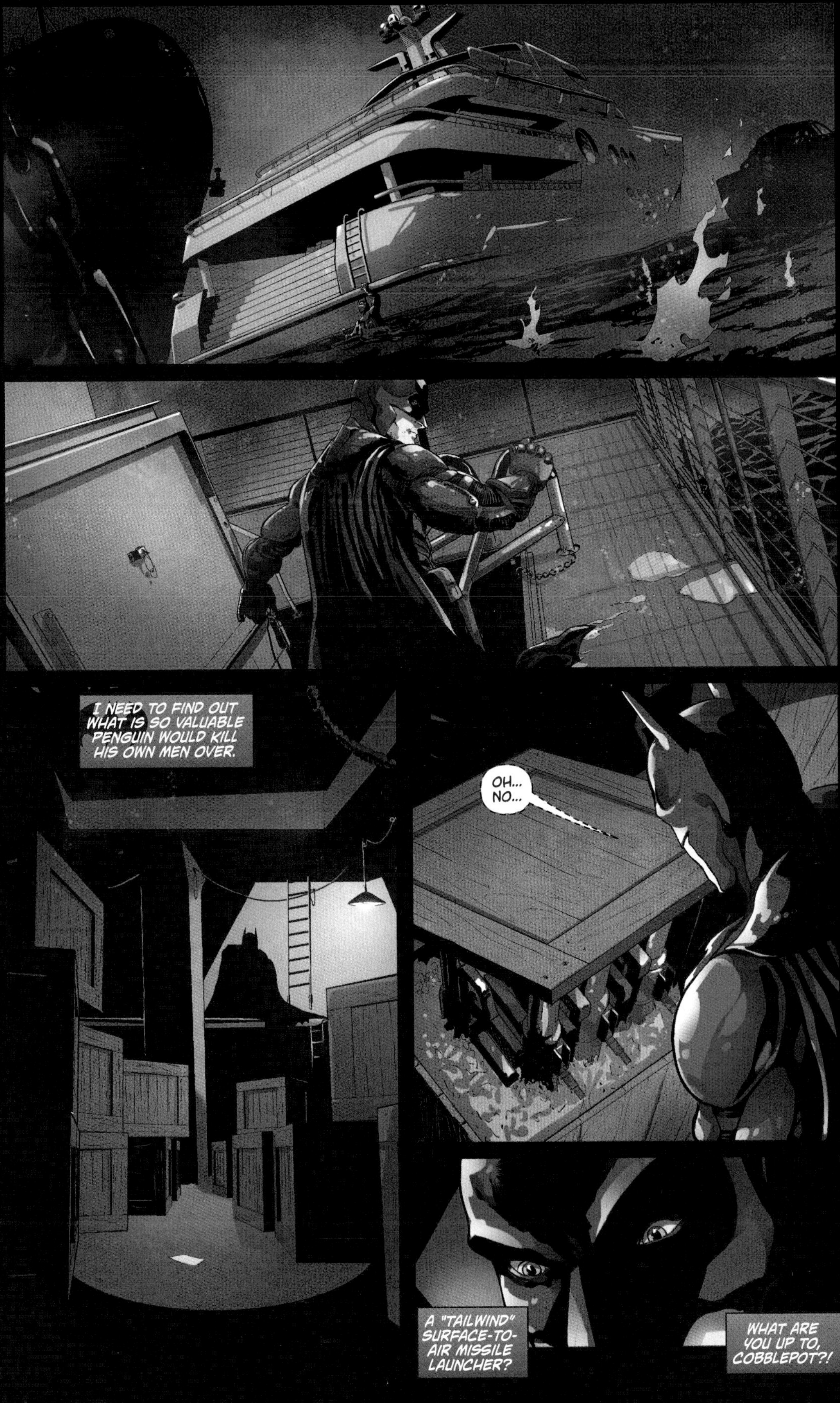
I NEED TO FIND OUT WHAT IS SO VALUABLE PENGUIN WOULD KILL HIS OWN MEN OVER.
OH... NO...
A "TAILWIND" SURFACE-TO-AIR MISSILE LAUNCHER?
WHAT ARE YOU UP TO, COBBLEPOT?!

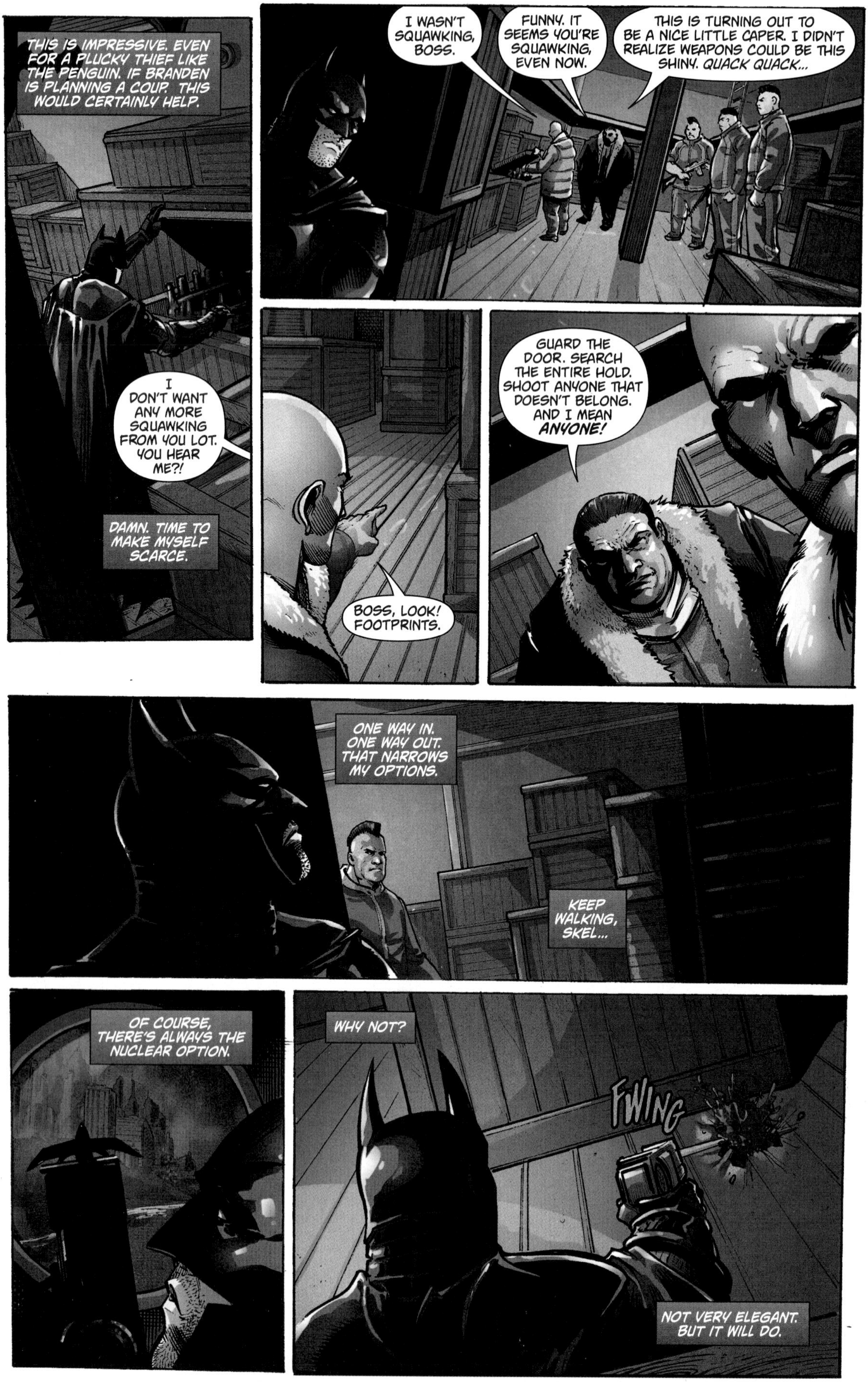
THIS IS IMPRESSIVE. EVEN FOR A PLUCKY THIEF LIKE THE PENGUIN. IF BRANDEN IS PLANNING A COUP, THIS WOULD CERTAINLY HELP.
I DON'T WANT ANY MORE SQUAWKING FROM YOU LOT. YOU HEAR ME?!
DAMN. TIME TO MAKE MYSELF SCARCE.
I WASN'T SQUAWKING, BOSS.
FUNNY. IT SEEMS YOU'RE SQUAWKING, EVEN NOW.
THIS IS TURNING OUT TO BE A NICE LITTLE CAPER. I DIDN'T REALIZE WEAPONS COULD BE THIS SHINY. QUACK QUACK...
BOSS, LOOK! FOOTPRINTS.
GUARD THE DOOR. SEARCH THE ENTIRE HOLD. SHOOT ANYONE THAT DOESN'T BELONG. AND I MEAN ANYONE!
ONE WAY IN. ONE WAY OUT. THAT NARROWS MY OPTIONS.
KEEP WALKING, SKEL...
OF COURSE, THERE'S ALWAYS THE NUCLEAR OPTION.
WHY NOT?
FWING
NOT VERY ELEGANT. BUT IT WILL DO.

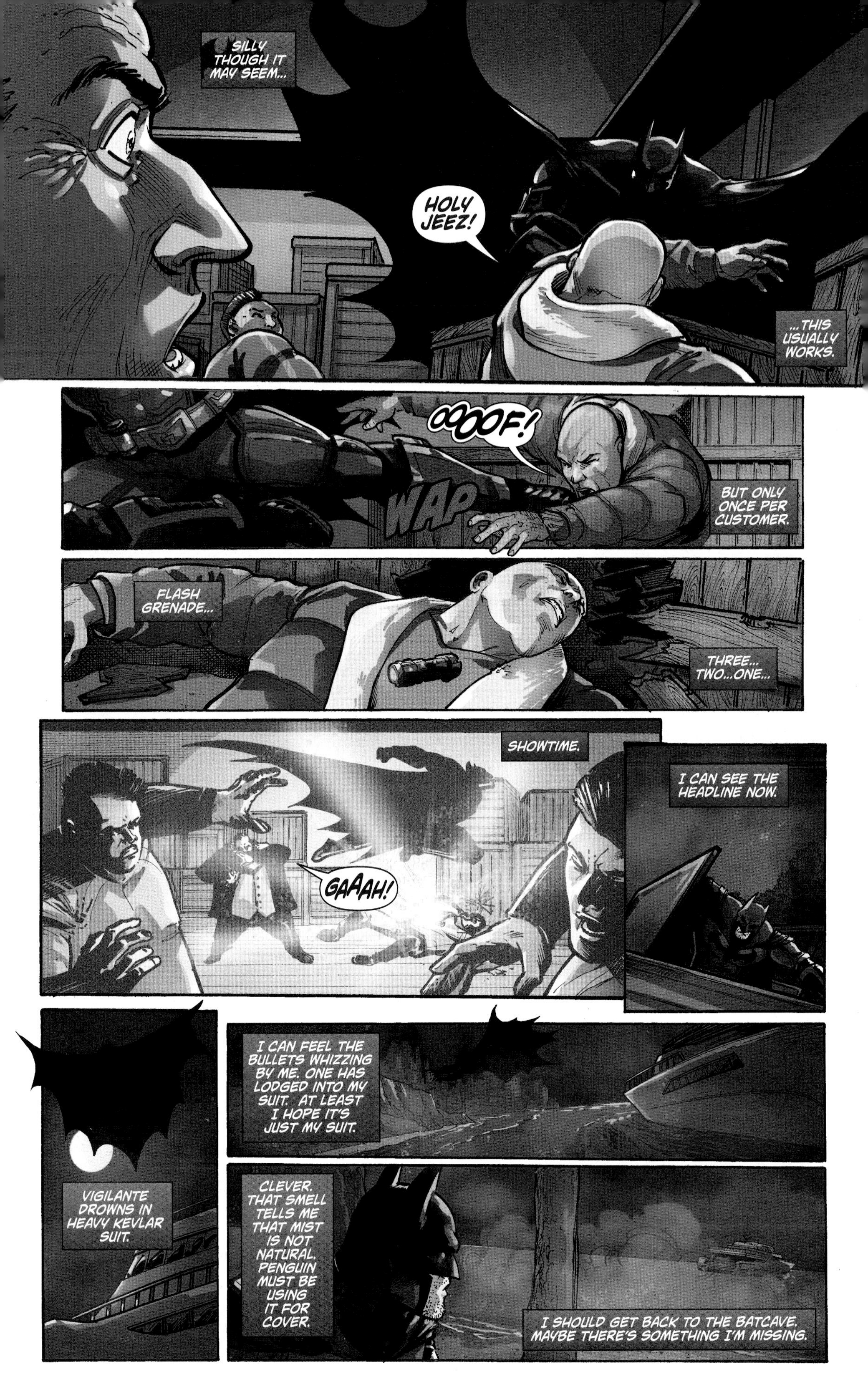
SILLY THOUGH IT MAY SEEM...
HOLY JEEZ!
...THIS USUALLY WORKS.
OOOOF!
WAP
BUT ONLY ONCE PER CUSTOMER.
FLASH GRENADE...
THREE... TWO...ONE...
SHOWTIME.
GAAAH!
I CAN SEE THE HEADLINE NOW.
VIGILANTE DROWNS IN HEAVY KEVLAR SUIT.
I CAN FEEL THE BULLETS WHIZZING BY ME. ONE HAS LODGED INTO MY SUIT. AT LEAST I HOPE IT'S JUST MY SUIT.
CLEVER. THAT SMELL TELLS ME THAT MIST IS NOT NATURAL. PENGUIN MUST BE USING IT FOR COVER.
I SHOULD GET BACK TO THE BATCAVE. MAYBE THERE'S SOMETHING I'M MISSING.

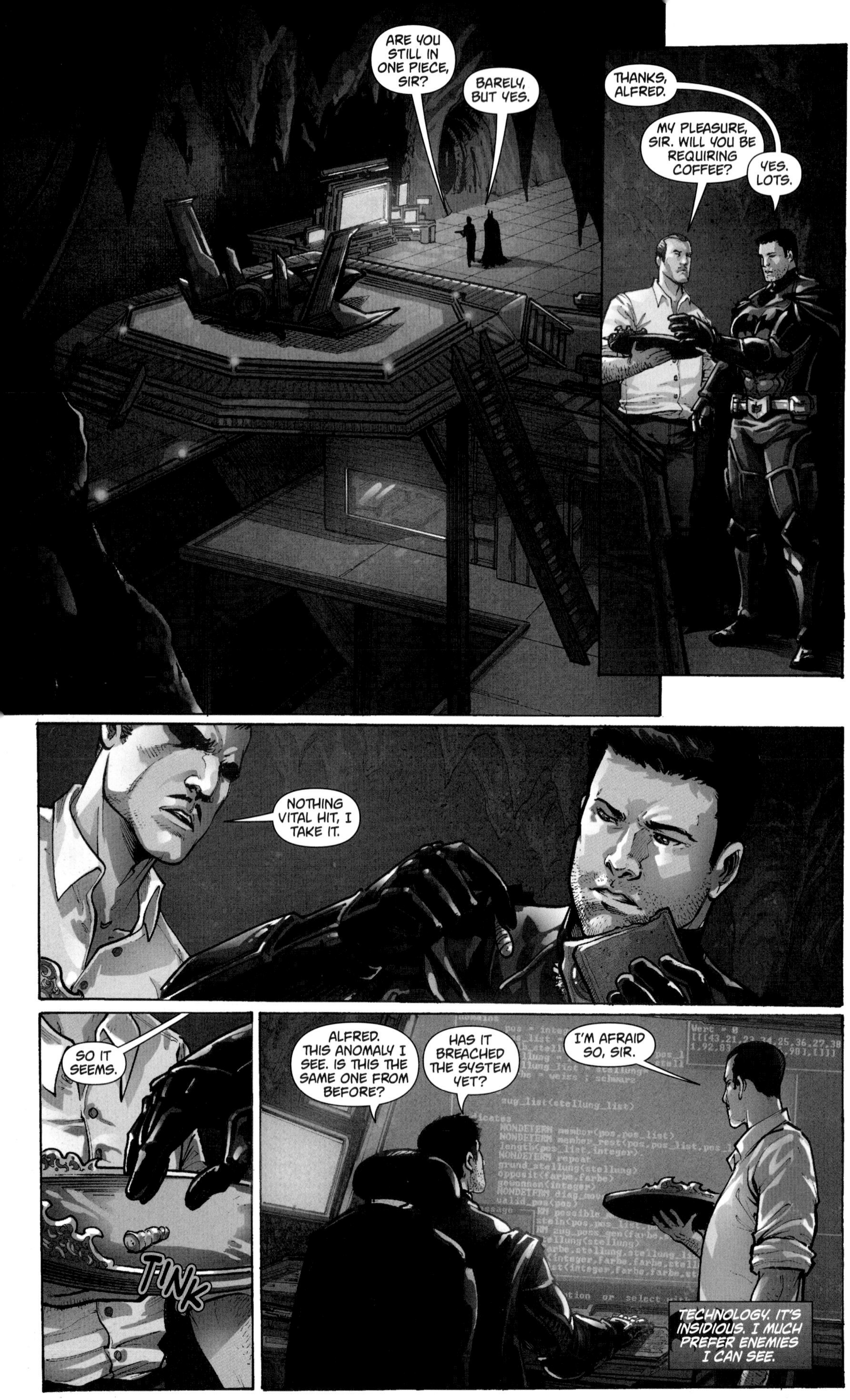
ARE YOU STILL IN ONE PIECE, SIR?
BARELY, BUT YES.
THANKS, ALFRED.
MY PLEASURE, SIR. WILL YOU BE REQUIRING COFFEE?
YES. LOTS.
NOTHING VITAL HIT, I TAKE IT.
SO IT SEEMS.
TINK
ALFRED. THIS ANOMALY I SEE. IS THIS THE SAME ONE FROM BEFORE?
HAS IT BREACHED THE SYSTEM YET?
I'M AFRAID SO, SIR.
TECHNOLOGY. IT'S INSIDIOUS. I MUCH PREFER ENEMIES I CAN SEE.

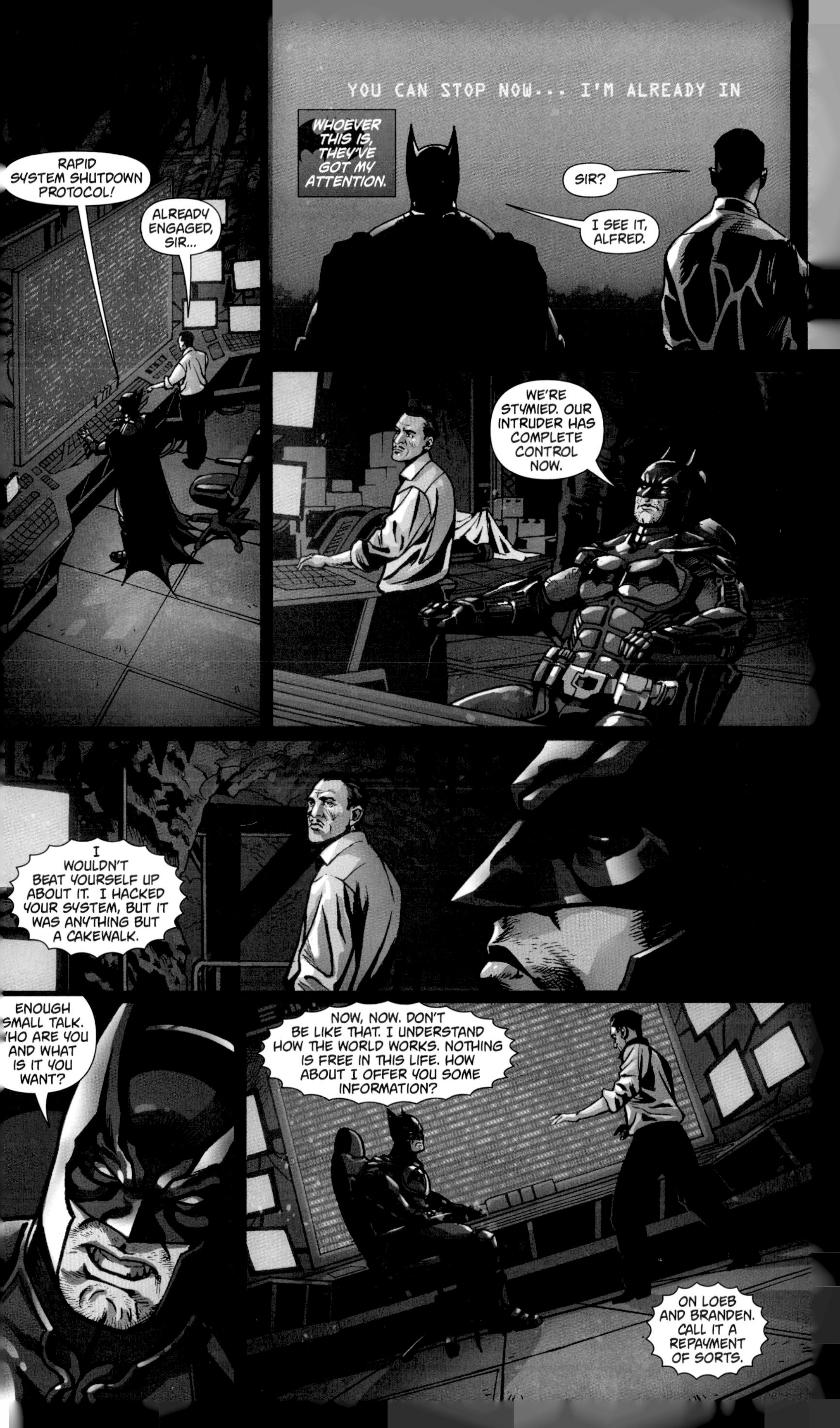
RAPID SYSTEM SHUTDOWN PROTOCOL!
ALREADY ENGAGED, SIR...
YOU CAN STOP NOW... I'M ALREADY IN
WHOEVER THIS IS, THEY'VE GOT MY ATTENTION.
SIR?
I SEE IT, ALFRED.
WE'RE STYMIED. OUR INTRUDER HAS COMPLETE CONTROL NOW.
I WOULDN'T BEAT YOURSELF UP ABOUT IT. I HACKED YOUR SYSTEM, BUT IT WAS ANYTHING BUT A CAKEWALK.
ENOUGH SMALL TALK. WHO ARE YOU AND WHAT IS IT YOU WANT?
NOW, NOW. DON'T BE LIKE THAT. I UNDERSTAND HOW THE WORLD WORKS. NOTHING IS FREE IN THIS LIFE. HOW ABOUT I OFFER YOU SOME INFORMATION?
ON LOEB AND BRANDEN. CALL IT A REPAYMENT OF SORTS.

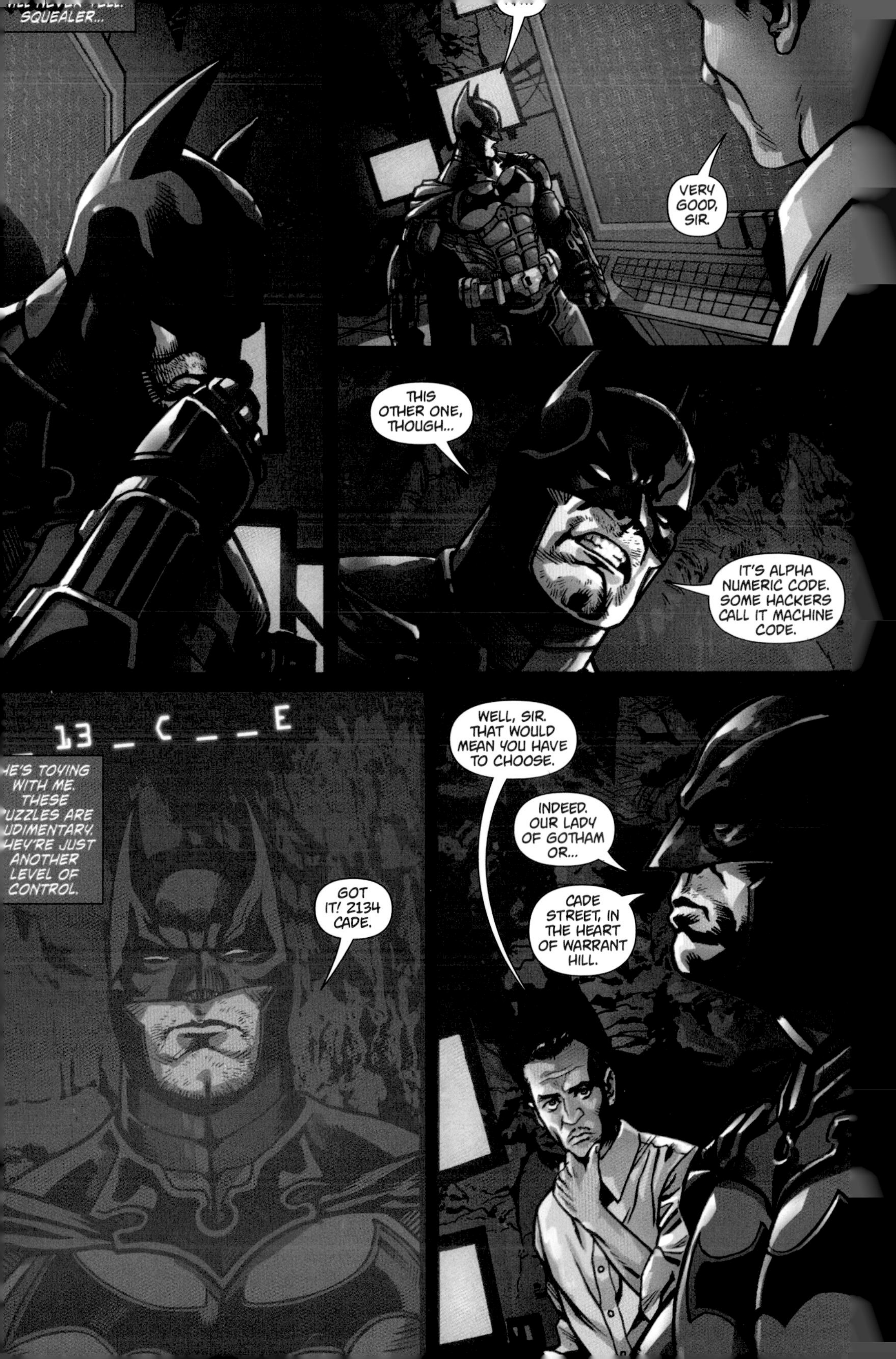

SQUEALER...
VERY GOOD, SIR.
THIS OTHER ONE, THOUGH...
IT'S ALPHA NUMERIC CODE. SOME HACKERS CALL IT MACHINE CODE.
13 _ C _ _ E
E'S TOYING WITH ME. THESE UZZLES ARE UDIMENTARY. HEY'RE JUST ANOTHER LEVEL OF CONTROL.
GOT IT! 2134 CADE.
WELL, SIR. THAT WOULD MEAN YOU HAVE TO CHOOSE.
INDEED. OUR LADY OF GOTHAM OR...
CADE STREET, IN THE HEART OF WARRANT HILL.

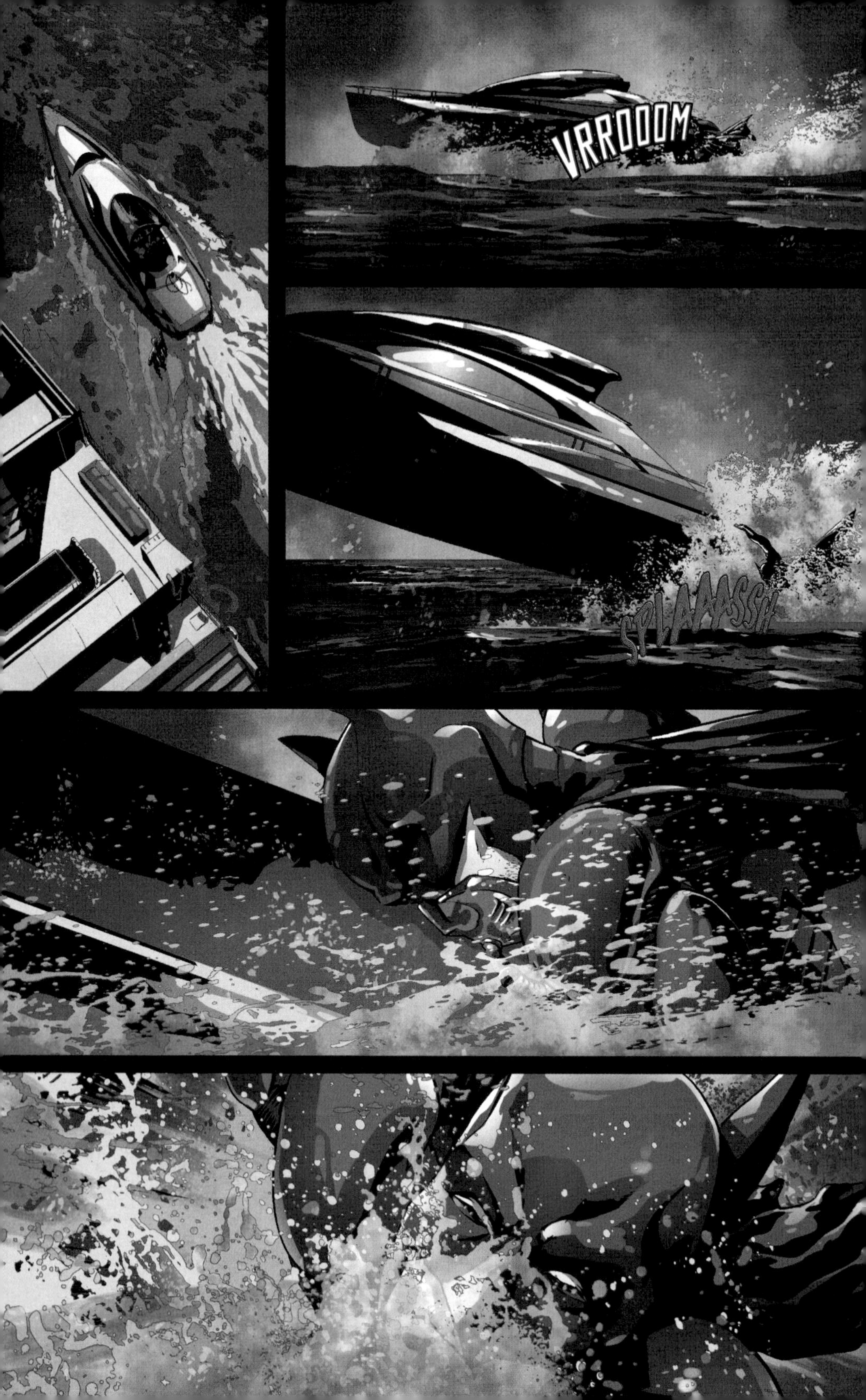
VRROOOM
SPLAAASSH

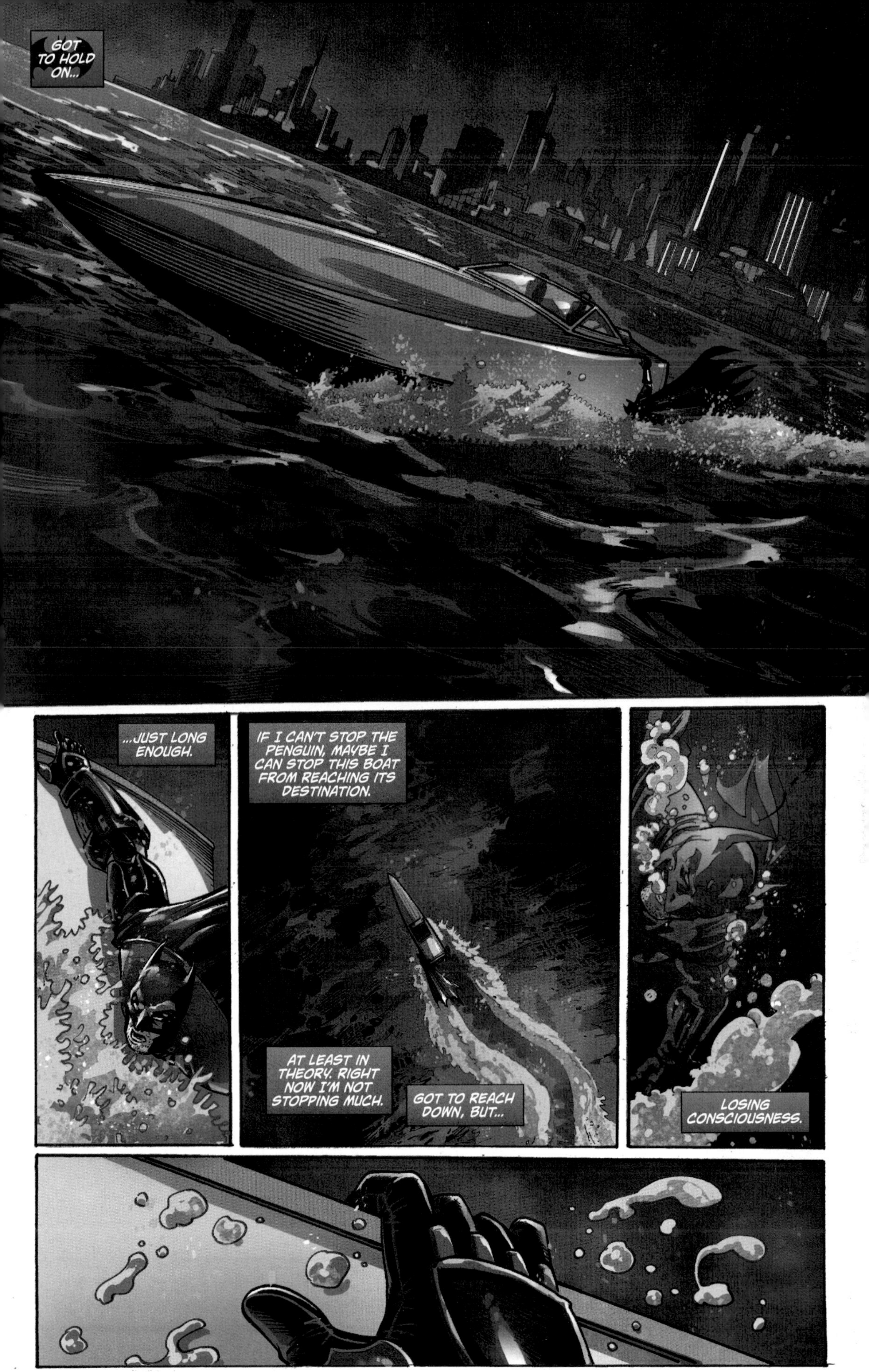
GOT TO HOLD ON...
...JUST LONG ENOUGH.
IF I CAN'T STOP THE PENGUIN, MAYBE I CAN STOP THIS BOAT FROM REACHING ITS DESTINATION.
AT LEAST IN THEORY. RIGHT NOW I'M NOT STOPPING MUCH.
GOT TO REACH DOWN, BUT...
LOSING CONSCIOUSNESS.

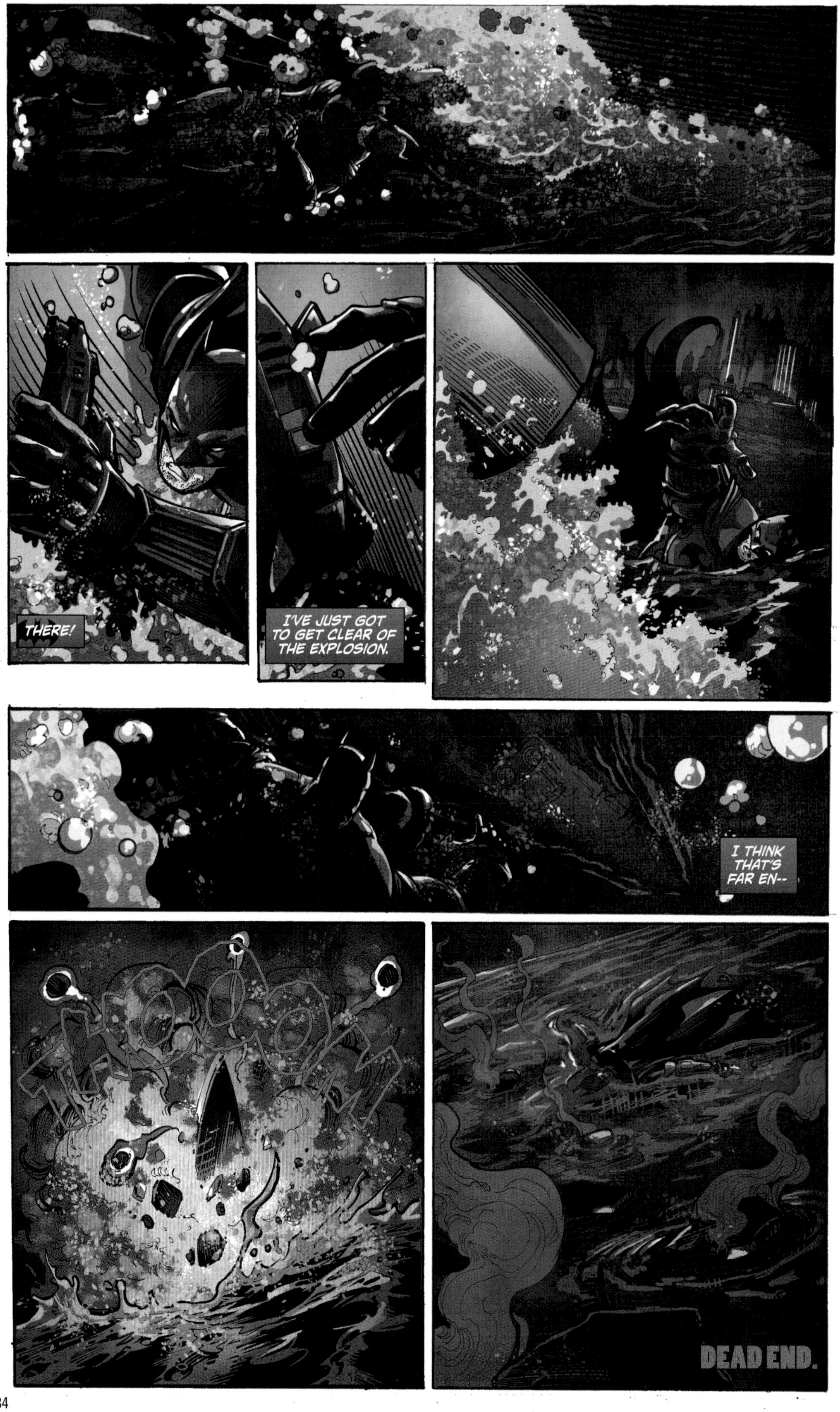
THERE!
I'VE JUST GOT TO GET CLEAR OF THE EXPLOSION.
I THINK THAT'S FAR EN--
DEAD END.

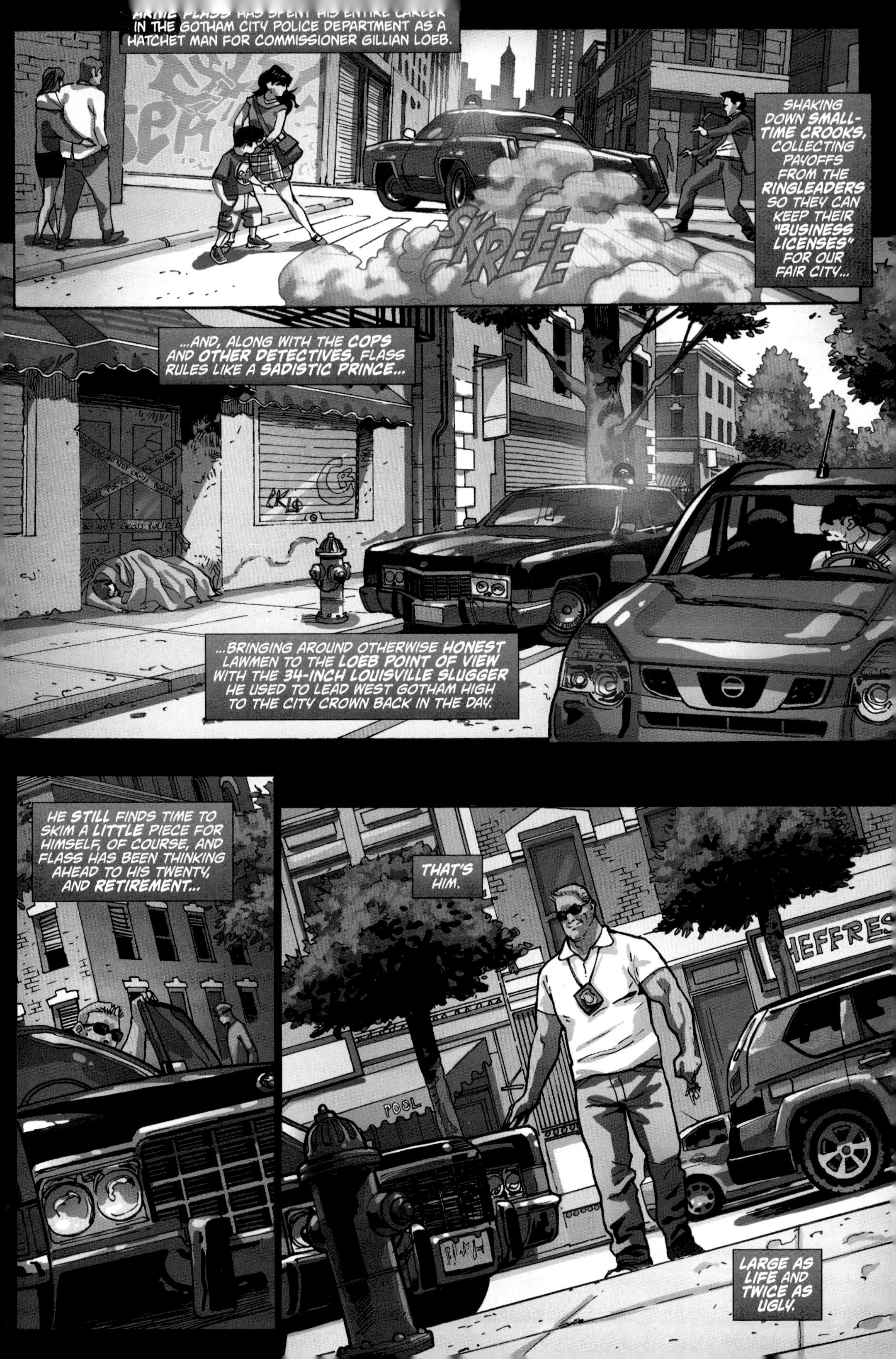
ARNIE FLASS HAS SPENT HIS ENTIRE CAREER IN THE GOTHAM CITY POLICE DEPARTMENT AS A HATCHET MAN FOR COMMISSIONER GILLIAN LOEB.
SKREEE
SHAKING DOWN SMALL-TIME CROOKS, COLLECTING PAYOFFS FROM THE RINGLEADERS SO THEY CAN KEEP THEIR "BUSINESS LICENSES" FOR OUR FAIR CITY...
...AND, ALONG WITH THE COPS AND OTHER DETECTIVES, FLASS RULES LIKE A SADISTIC PRINCE...
...BRINGING AROUND OTHERWISE HONEST LAWMEN TO THE LOEB POINT OF VIEW WITH THE 34-INCH LOUISVILLE SLUGGER HE USED TO LEAD WEST GOTHAM HIGH TO THE CITY CROWN BACK IN THE DAY.
HE STILL FINDS TIME TO SKIM A LITTLE PIECE FOR HIMSELF, OF COURSE, AND FLASS HAS BEEN THINKING AHEAD TO HIS TWENTY, AND RETIREMENT...
THAT'S HIM.
POOL
LARGE AS LIFE AND TWICE AS UGLY.

TO TALK YOUR WAY OUT, CONTINUE TO NEXT PAGE. TO FIGHT YOUR WAY OUT, SKIP TO PAGE 53.

IT'S TOO EARLY TO SHOW MY HAND TO FLASS. HE'S WELL KNOWN FOR HIS RESISTANCE TO INTIMIDATION, CONFRONTING HIM HERE AND NOW WILL LIKELY GET ME NOWHERE.

ALFRED, FIND OUT EVERYTHING YOU CAN ABOUT AN EXTREMELY LARGE MAN THAT GOES BY THE NAME "DUMPLER."

I'M RUNNING IT NOW, SIR.

THE MAN YOU ARE LOOKING FOR IS HUMPHREY DUMPLER. HIS POLICE RECORD IS QUITE LENGTHY, SIR.

HIS FILE INDICATES HE WORKS STRICTLY AS HIRED MUSCLE. HE APPEARS TO BE QUITE FORMIDABLE IN COMBAT, BUT NOT PARTICULARLY BRIGHT.

BUT I AM CONCERNED ABOUT THIS BEHEMOTH HE'S ASSOCIATING WITH. I NEED MORE INFORMATION.

THANK YOU, ALFRED.

FLASS UNDOUBTEDLY SEES DUMPLER AS THE IDEAL PATSY, AND I DOUBT DUMPLER KNOWS MUCH ABOUT THE ENTIRE SCOPE OF FLASS' PLANS.

FLASS IS MY ONLY WAY IN.

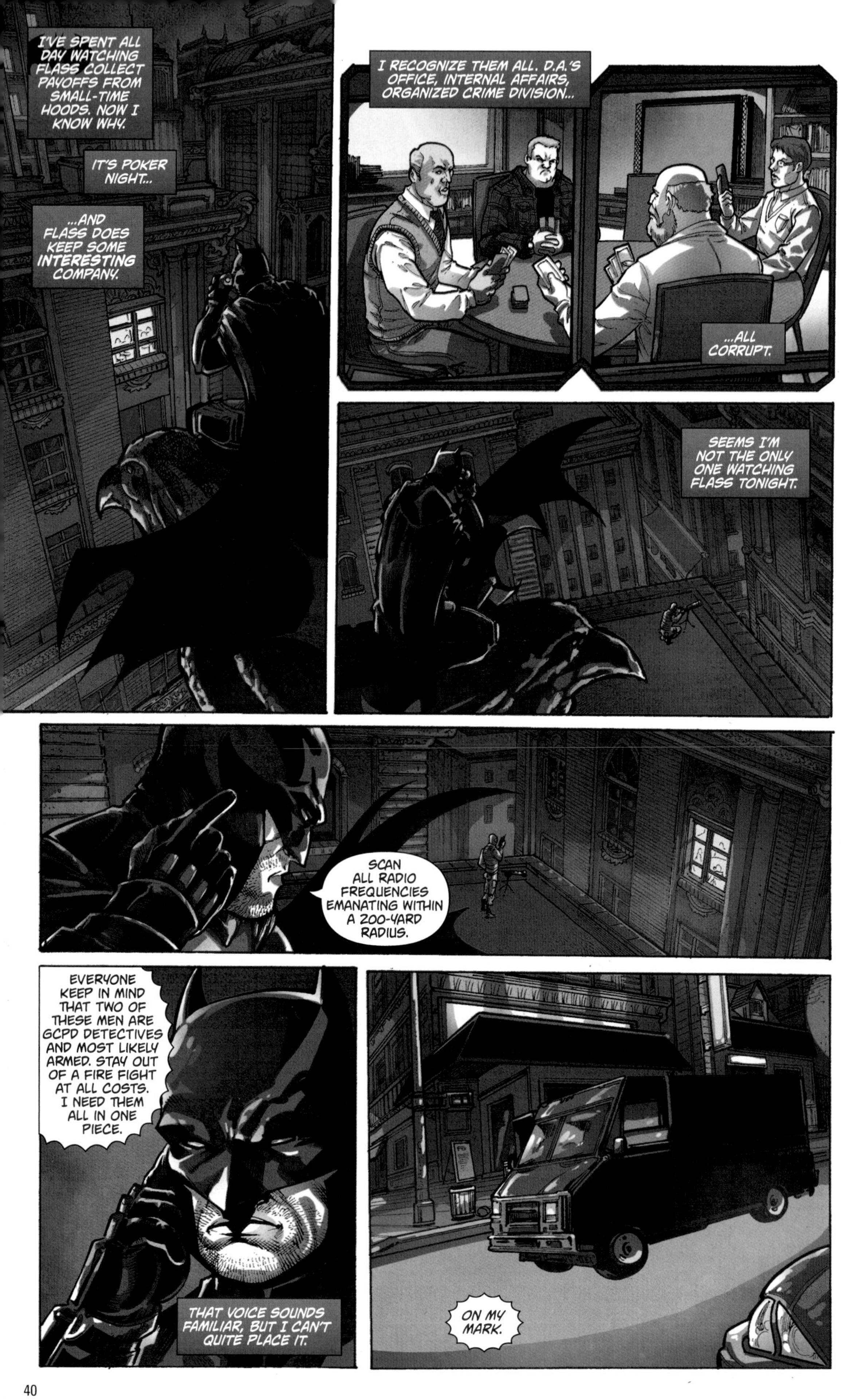
I'VE SPENT ALL DAY WATCHING FLASS COLLECT PAYOFFS FROM SMALL-TIME HOODS. NOW I KNOW WHY.
IT'S POKER NIGHT...
...AND FLASS DOES KEEP SOME INTERESTING COMPANY.
I RECOGNIZE THEM ALL. D.A.'S OFFICE, INTERNAL AFFAIRS, ORGANIZED CRIME DIVISION...
...ALL CORRUPT.
SEEMS I'M NOT THE ONLY ONE WATCHING FLASS TONIGHT.
SCAN ALL RADIO FREQUENCIES EMANATING WITHIN A 200-YARD RADIUS.
EVERYONE KEEP IN MIND THAT TWO OF THESE MEN ARE GCPD DETECTIVES AND MOST LIKELY ARMED. STAY OUT OF A FIRE FIGHT AT ALL COSTS. I NEED THEM ALL IN ONE PIECE.
THAT VOICE SOUNDS FAMILIAR, BUT I CAN'T QUITE PLACE IT.
ON MY MARK.

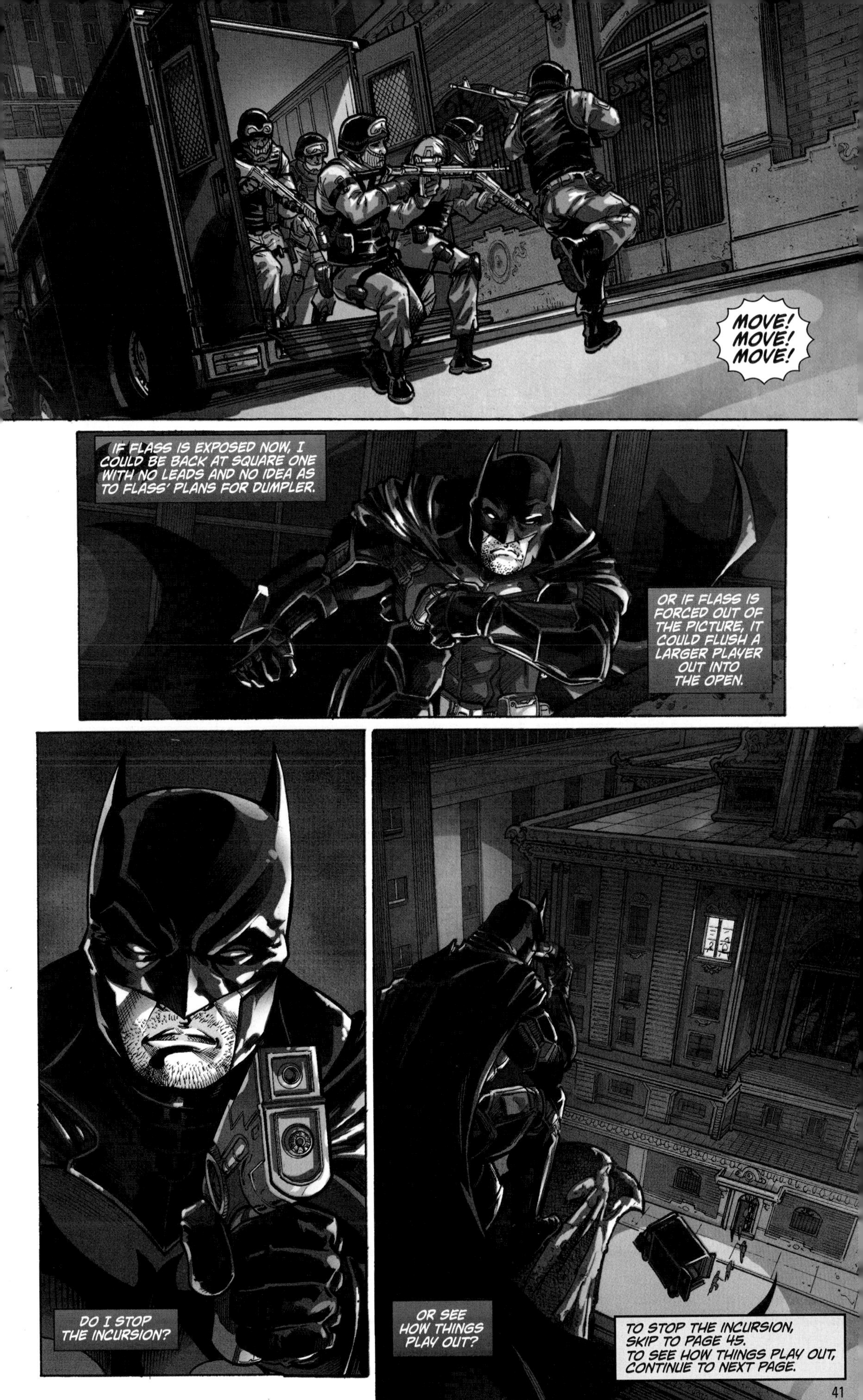
MOVE! MOVE! MOVE!
IF FLASS IS EXPOSED NOW, I COULD BE BACK AT SQUARE ONE WITH NO LEADS AND NO IDEA AS TO FLASS' PLANS FOR DUMPLER.
OR IF FLASS IS FORCED OUT OF THE PICTURE, IT COULD FLUSH A LARGER PLAYER OUT INTO THE OPEN.
DO I STOP THE INCURSION?
OR SEE HOW THINGS PLAY OUT?
TO STOP THE INCURSION, SKIP TO PAGE 45.
TO SEE HOW THINGS PLAY OUT, CONTINUE TO NEXT PAGE.

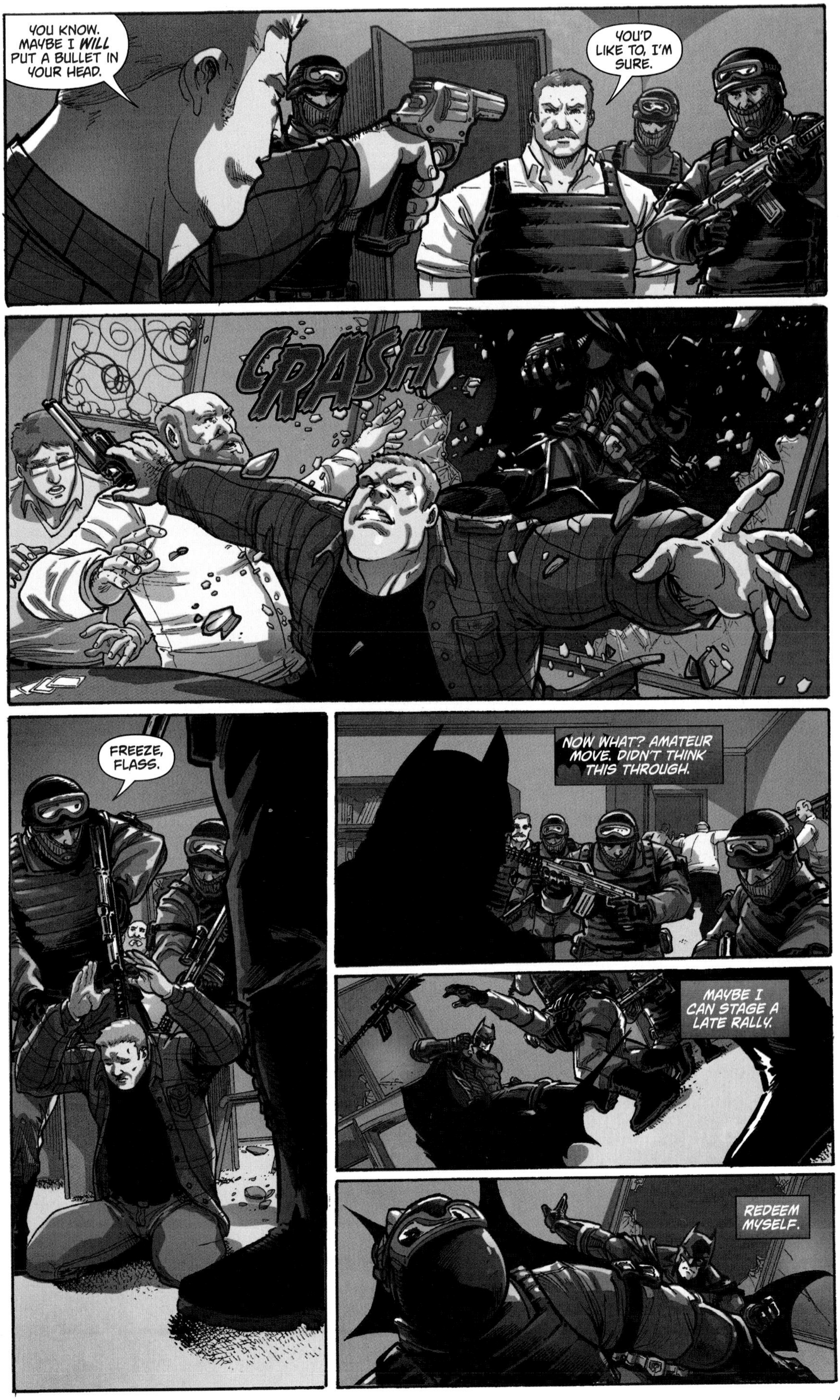
YOU KNOW. MAYBE I WILL PUT A BULLET IN YOUR HEAD.
YOU'D LIKE TO, I'M SURE.
CRASH
FREEZE, FLASS.
NOW WHAT? AMATEUR MOVE. DIDN'T THINK THIS THROUGH.
MAYBE I CAN STAGE A LATE RALLY.
REDEEM MYSELF.

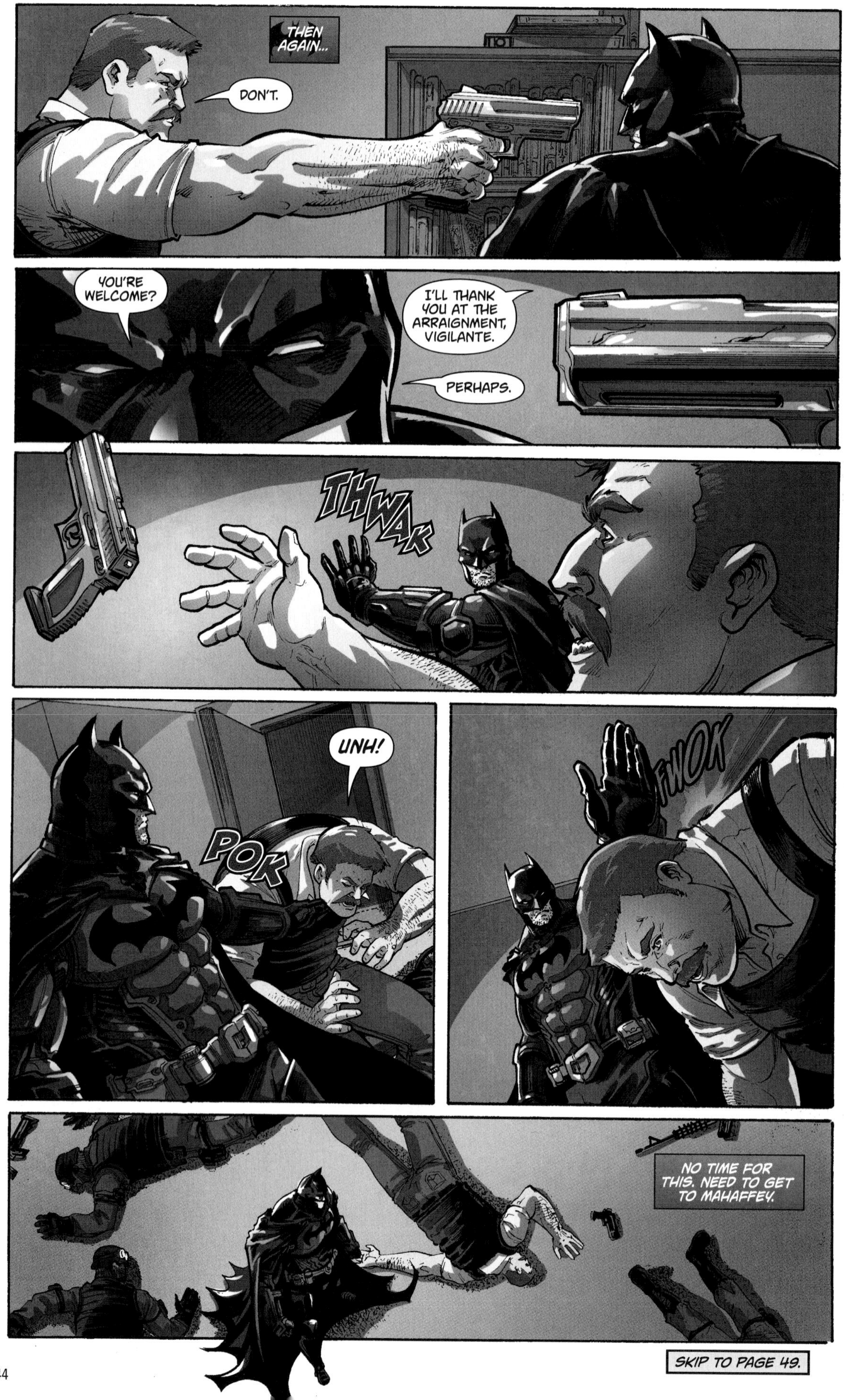
THEN AGAIN...
DON'T.
YOU'RE WELCOME?
I'LL THANK YOU AT THE ARRAIGNMENT, VIGILANTE.
PERHAPS.
THWAK
UNH!
POK
FWOK
NO TIME FOR THIS. NEED TO GET TO MAHAFFEY.

SKIP TO PAGE 49.

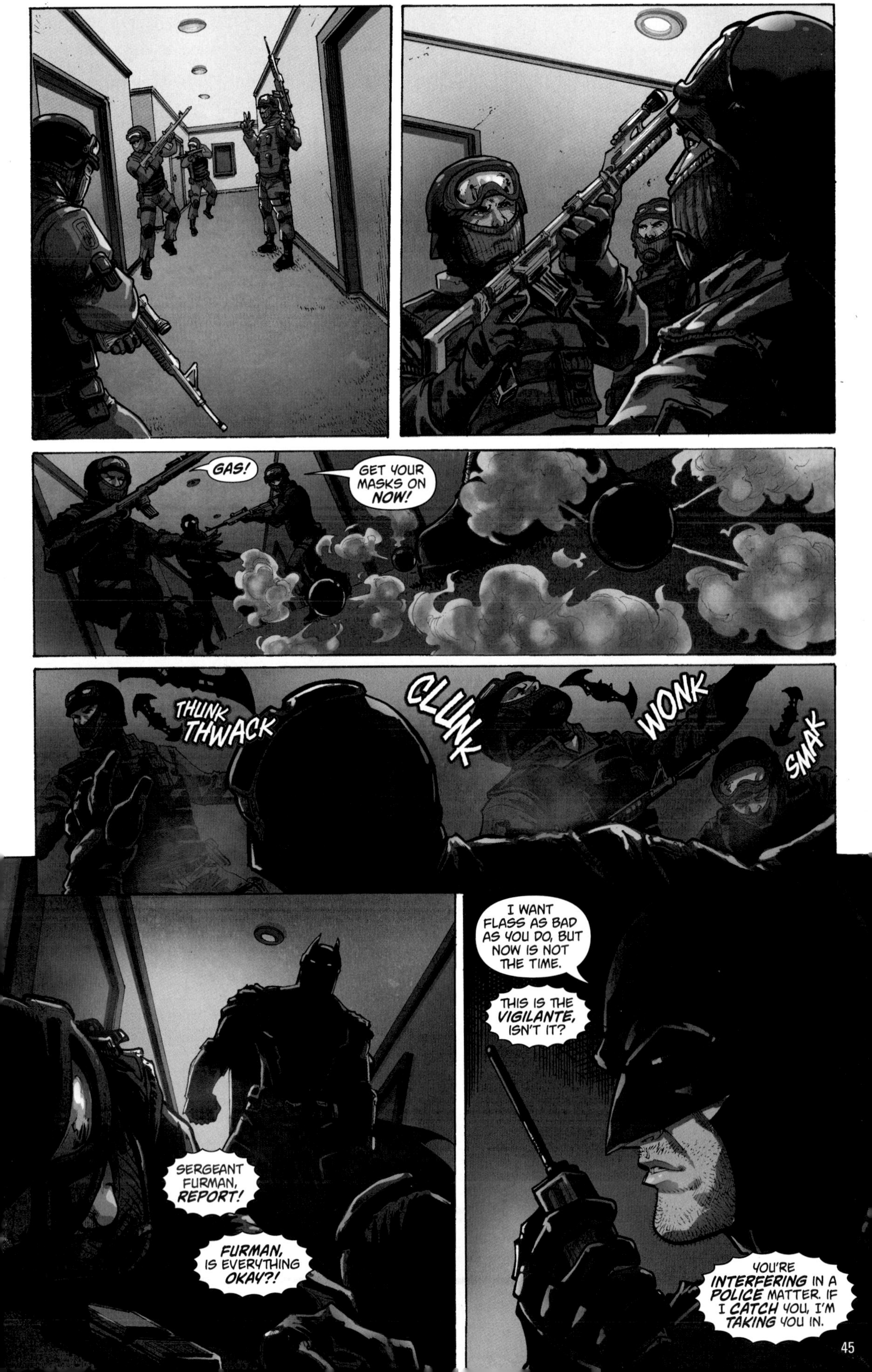
GAS!
GET YOUR MASKS ON NOW!
THUNK
THWACK
CLUNK
WONK
SMAK
SERGEANT FURMAN, REPORT!
FURMAN, IS EVERYTHING OKAY?!
I WANT FLASS AS BAD AS YOU DO, BUT NOW IS NOT THE TIME.
THIS IS THE VIGILANTE, ISN'T IT?
YOU'RE INTERFERING IN A POLICE MATTER. IF I CATCH YOU, I'M TAKING YOU IN.

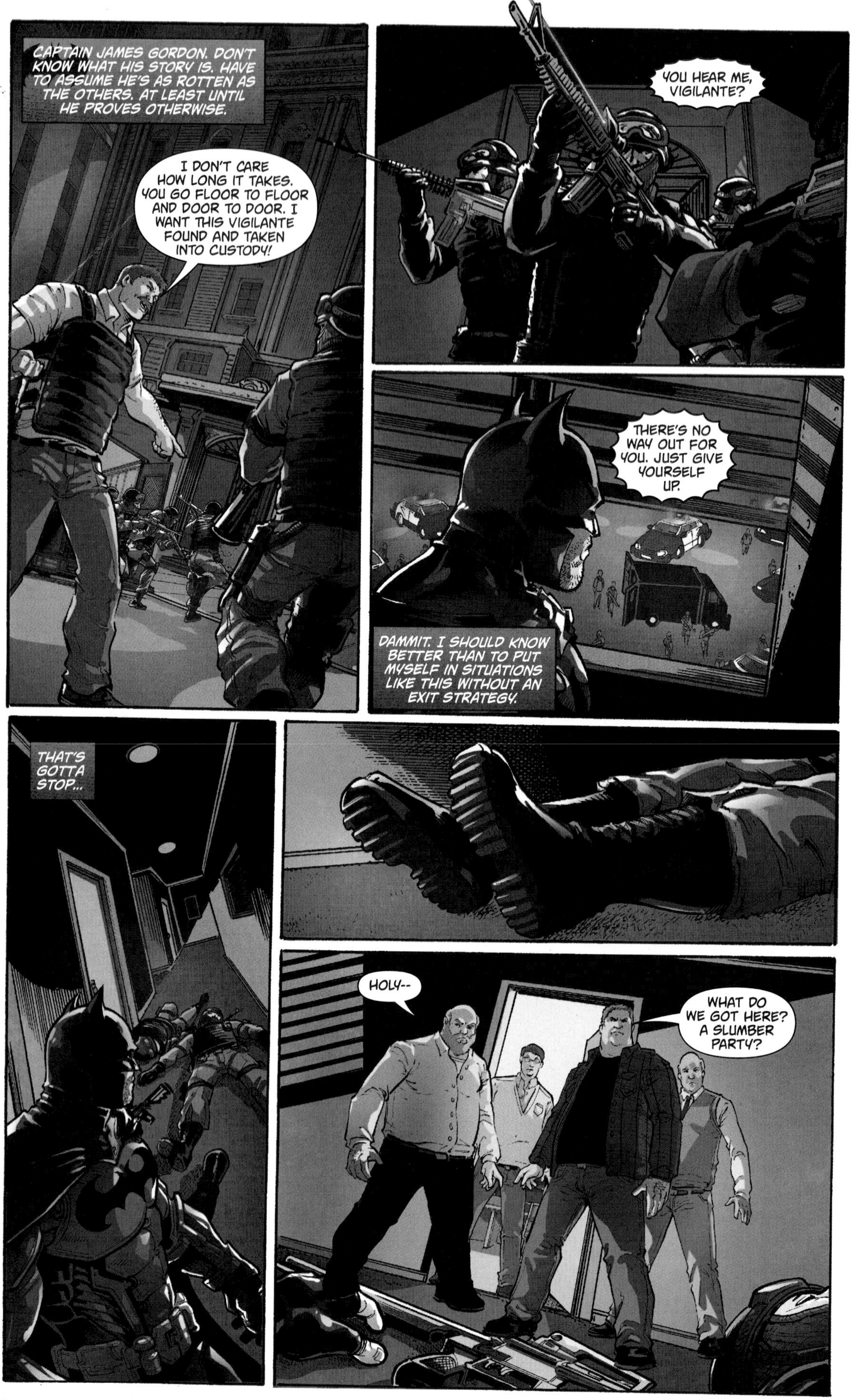
CAPTAIN JAMES GORDON. DON'T KNOW WHAT HIS STORY IS. HAVE TO ASSUME HE'S AS ROTTEN AS THE OTHERS. AT LEAST UNTIL HE PROVES OTHERWISE.
I DON'T CARE HOW LONG IT TAKES. YOU GO FLOOR TO FLOOR AND DOOR TO DOOR. I WANT THIS VIGILANTE FOUND AND TAKEN INTO CUSTODY!
YOU HEAR ME, VIGILANTE?
THERE'S NO WAY OUT FOR YOU. JUST GIVE YOURSELF UP.
DAMMIT. I SHOULD KNOW BETTER THAN TO PUT MYSELF IN SITUATIONS LIKE THIS WITHOUT AN EXIT STRATEGY.
THAT'S GOTTA STOP...
HOLY--
WHAT DO WE GOT HERE? A SLUMBER PARTY?

47

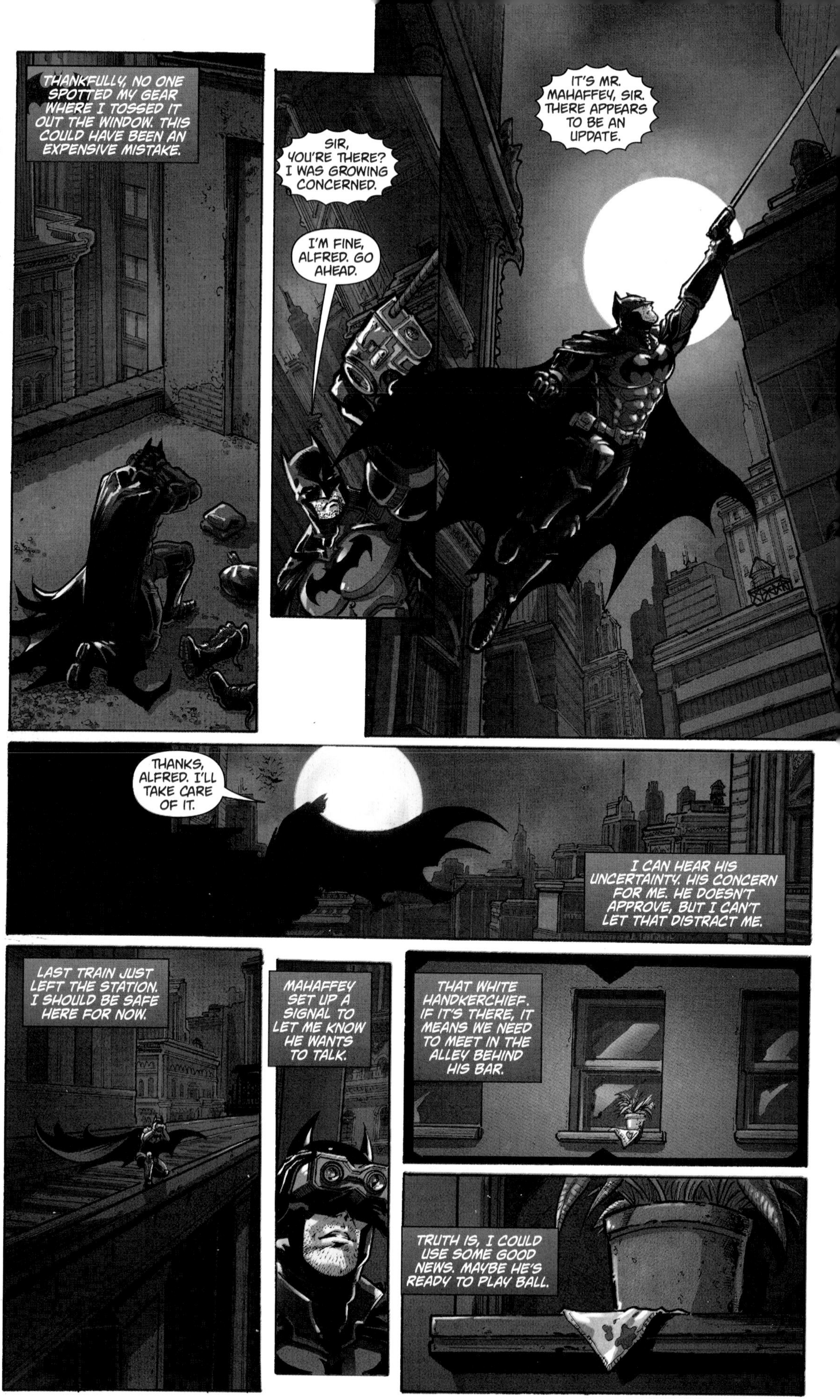
THANKFULLY, NO ONE SPOTTED MY GEAR WHERE I TOSSED IT OUT THE WINDOW. THIS COULD HAVE BEEN AN EXPENSIVE MISTAKE.
SIR, YOU'RE THERE? I WAS GROWING CONCERNED.
I'M FINE, ALFRED. GO AHEAD.
IT'S MR. MAHAFFEY, SIR. THERE APPEARS TO BE AN UPDATE.
THANKS, ALFRED. I'LL TAKE CARE OF IT.
I CAN HEAR HIS UNCERTAINTY. HIS CONCERN FOR ME. HE DOESN'T APPROVE, BUT I CAN'T LET THAT DISTRACT ME.
LAST TRAIN JUST LEFT THE STATION. I SHOULD BE SAFE HERE FOR NOW.
MAHAFFEY SET UP A SIGNAL TO LET ME KNOW HE WANTS TO TALK.
THAT WHITE HANDKERCHIEF. IF IT'S THERE, IT MEANS WE NEED TO MEET IN THE ALLEY BEHIND HIS BAR.
TRUTH IS, I COULD USE SOME GOOD NEWS. MAYBE HE'S READY TO PLAY BALL.

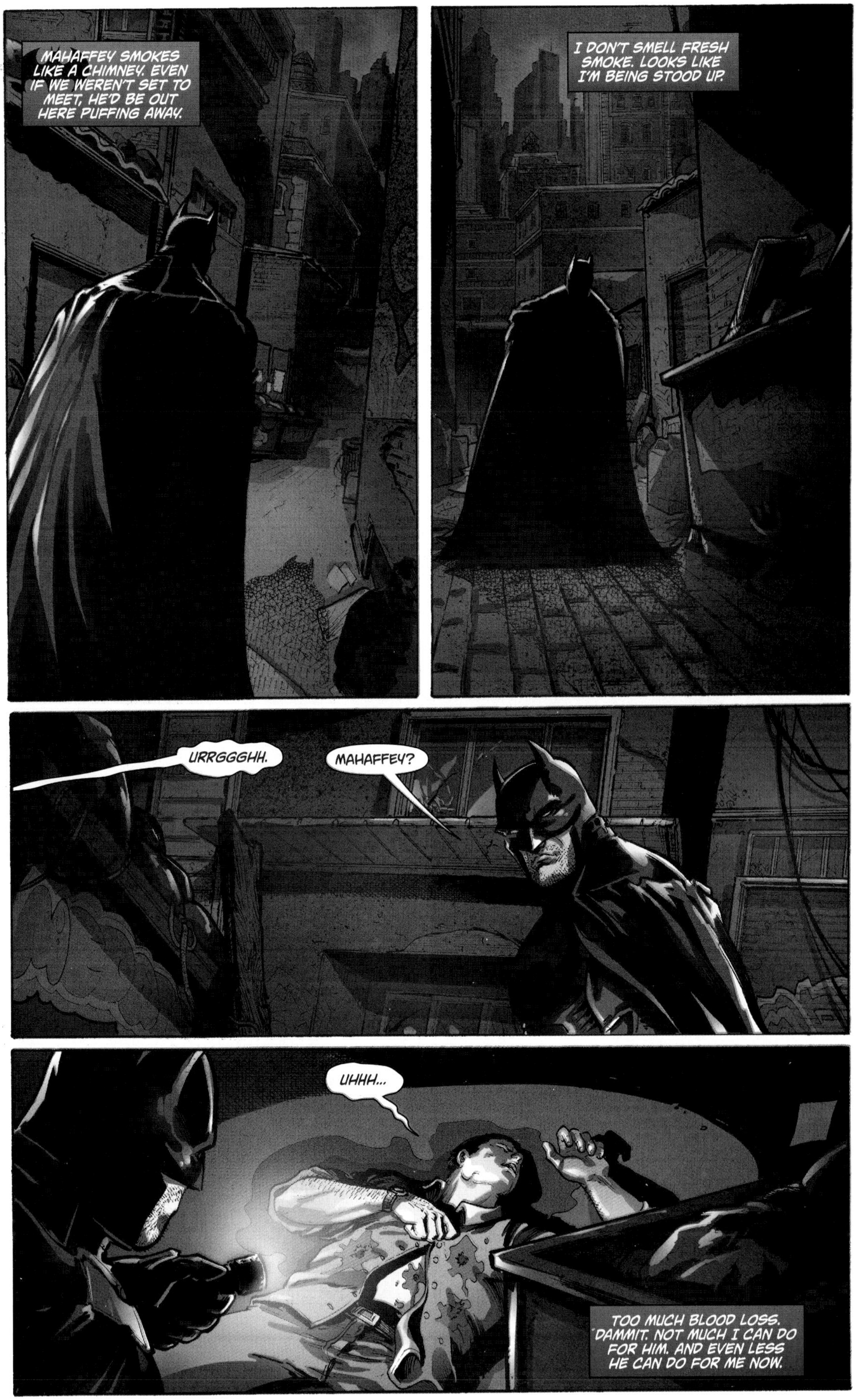
MAHAFFEY SMOKES LIKE A CHIMNEY. EVEN IF WE WEREN'T SET TO MEET, HE'D BE OUT HERE PUFFING AWAY.
I DON'T SMELL FRESH SMOKE. LOOKS LIKE I'M BEING STOOD UP.
URRGGGHH.
MAHAFFEY?
UHHH...
TOO MUCH BLOOD LOSS. DAMMIT. NOT MUCH I CAN DO FOR HIM. AND EVEN LESS HE CAN DO FOR ME NOW.

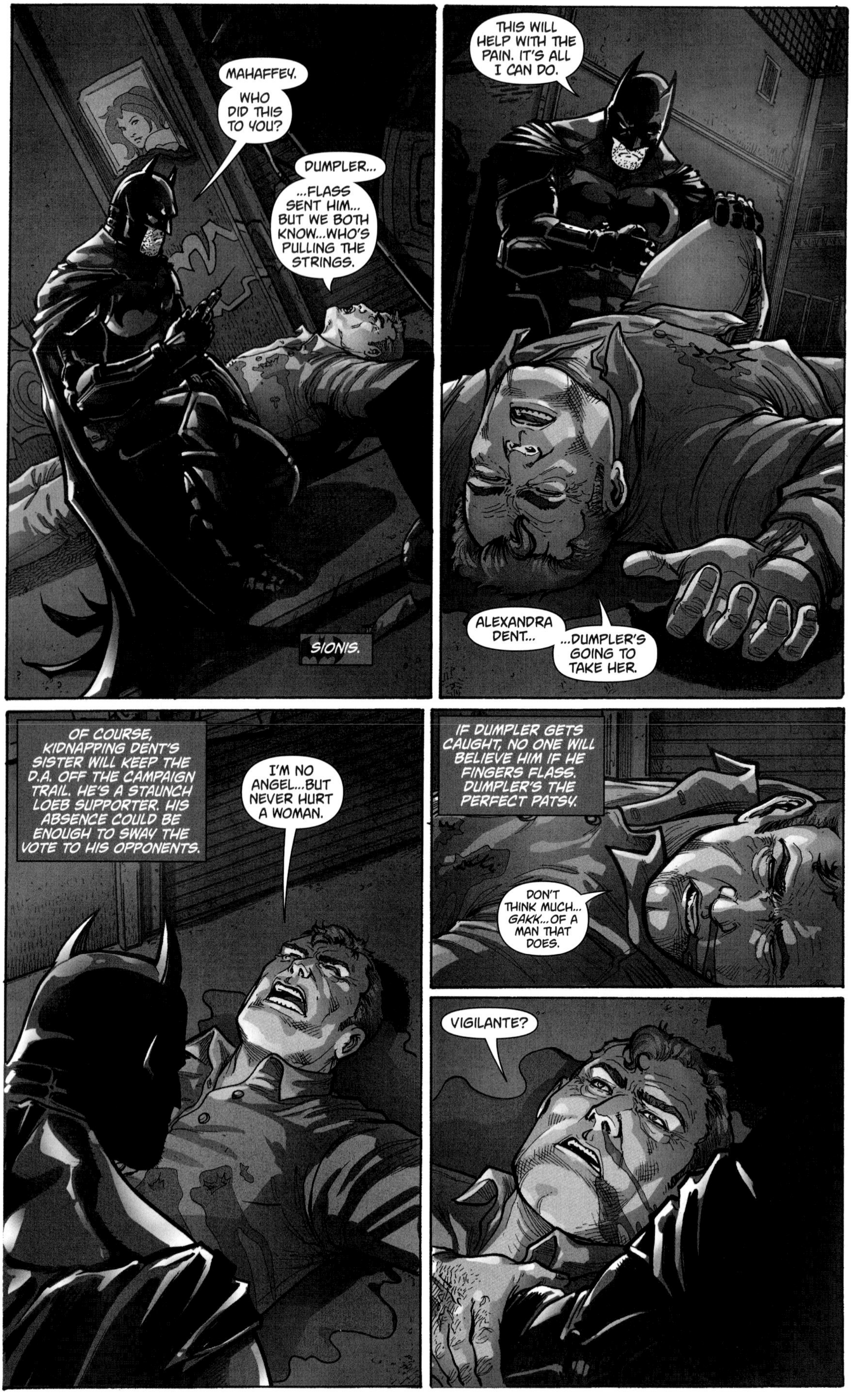
MAHAFFEY.
WHO DID THIS TO YOU?
DUMPLER...
...FLASS SENT HIM... BUT WE BOTH KNOW...WHO'S PULLING THE STRINGS.
SIONIS.
THIS WILL HELP WITH THE PAIN. IT'S ALL I CAN DO.
ALEXANDRA DENT...
...DUMPLER'S GOING TO TAKE HER.
OF COURSE, KIDNAPPING DENT'S SISTER WILL KEEP THE D.A. OFF THE CAMPAIGN TRAIL. HE'S A STAUNCH LOEB SUPPORTER. HIS ABSENCE COULD BE ENOUGH TO SWAY THE VOTE TO HIS OPPONENTS.
I'M NO ANGEL...BUT NEVER HURT A WOMAN.
IF DUMPLER GETS CAUGHT, NO ONE WILL BELIEVE HIM IF HE FINGERS FLASS. DUMPLER'S THE PERFECT PATSY.
DON'T THINK MUCH... GAKK...OF A MAN THAT DOES.
VIGILANTE?

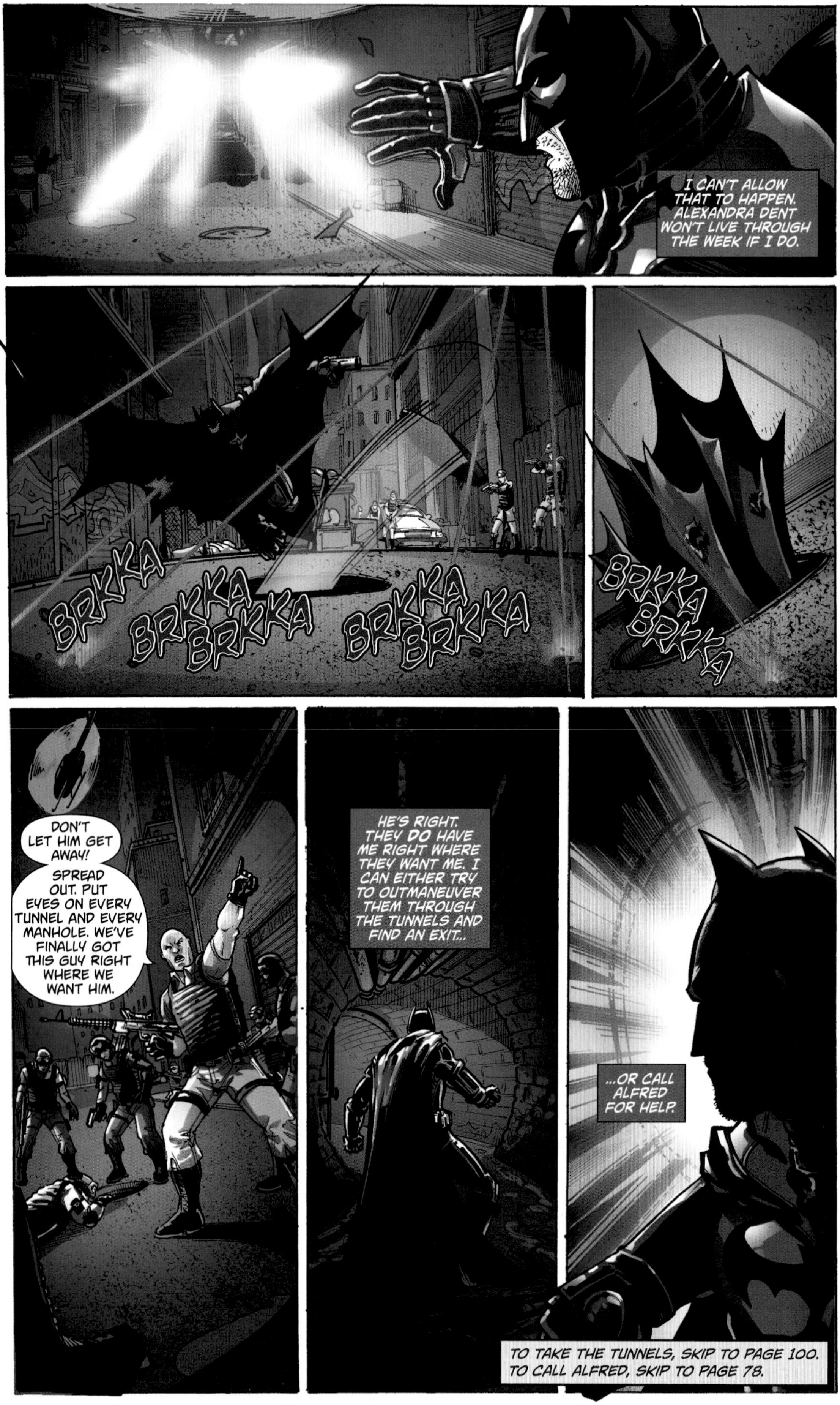
I CAN'T ALLOW THAT TO HAPPEN. ALEXANDRA DENT WON'T LIVE THROUGH THE WEEK IF I DO.
BRKKA BRKKA BRKKA BRKKA BRKKA
BRKKA BRKKA BRKKA
DON'T LET HIM GET AWAY!
SPREAD OUT. PUT EYES ON EVERY TUNNEL AND EVERY MANHOLE. WE'VE FINALLY GOT THIS GUY RIGHT WHERE WE WANT HIM.
HE'S RIGHT. THEY DO HAVE ME RIGHT WHERE THEY WANT ME. I CAN EITHER TRY TO OUTMANEUVER THEM THROUGH THE TUNNELS AND FIND AN EXIT...
...OR CALL ALFRED FOR HELP.
TO TAKE THE TUNNELS, SKIP TO PAGE 100.
TO CALL ALFRED, SKIP TO PAGE 78.

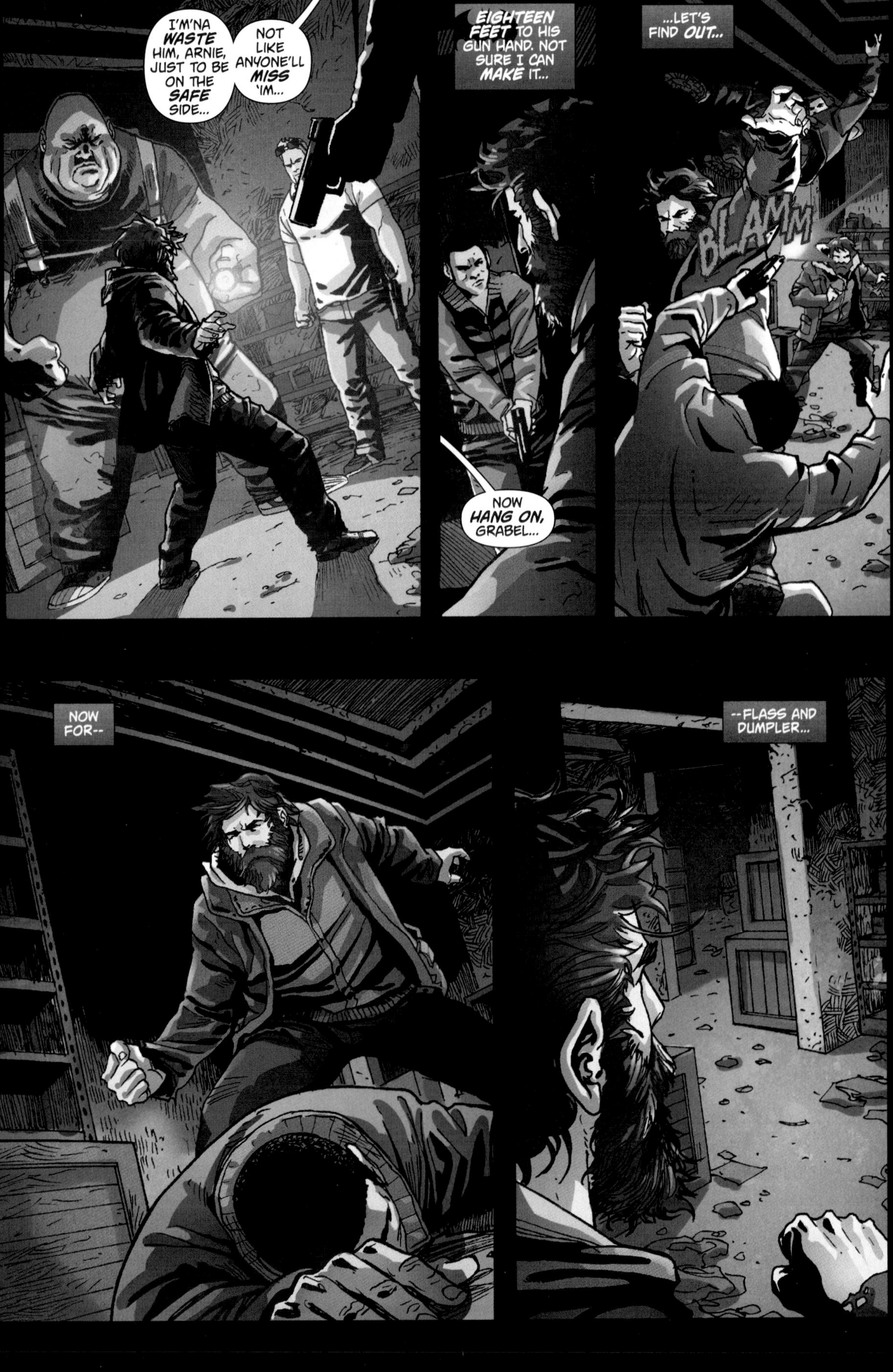
I'M'NA WASTE HIM, ARNIE, JUST TO BE ON THE SAFE SIDE...
NOT LIKE ANYONE'LL MISS 'IM...
EIGHTEEN FEET TO HIS GUN HAND. NOT SURE I CAN MAKE IT...
NOW HANG ON, GRABEL...
...LET'S FIND OUT...
BLAMM
NOW FOR--
--FLASS AND DUMPLER...

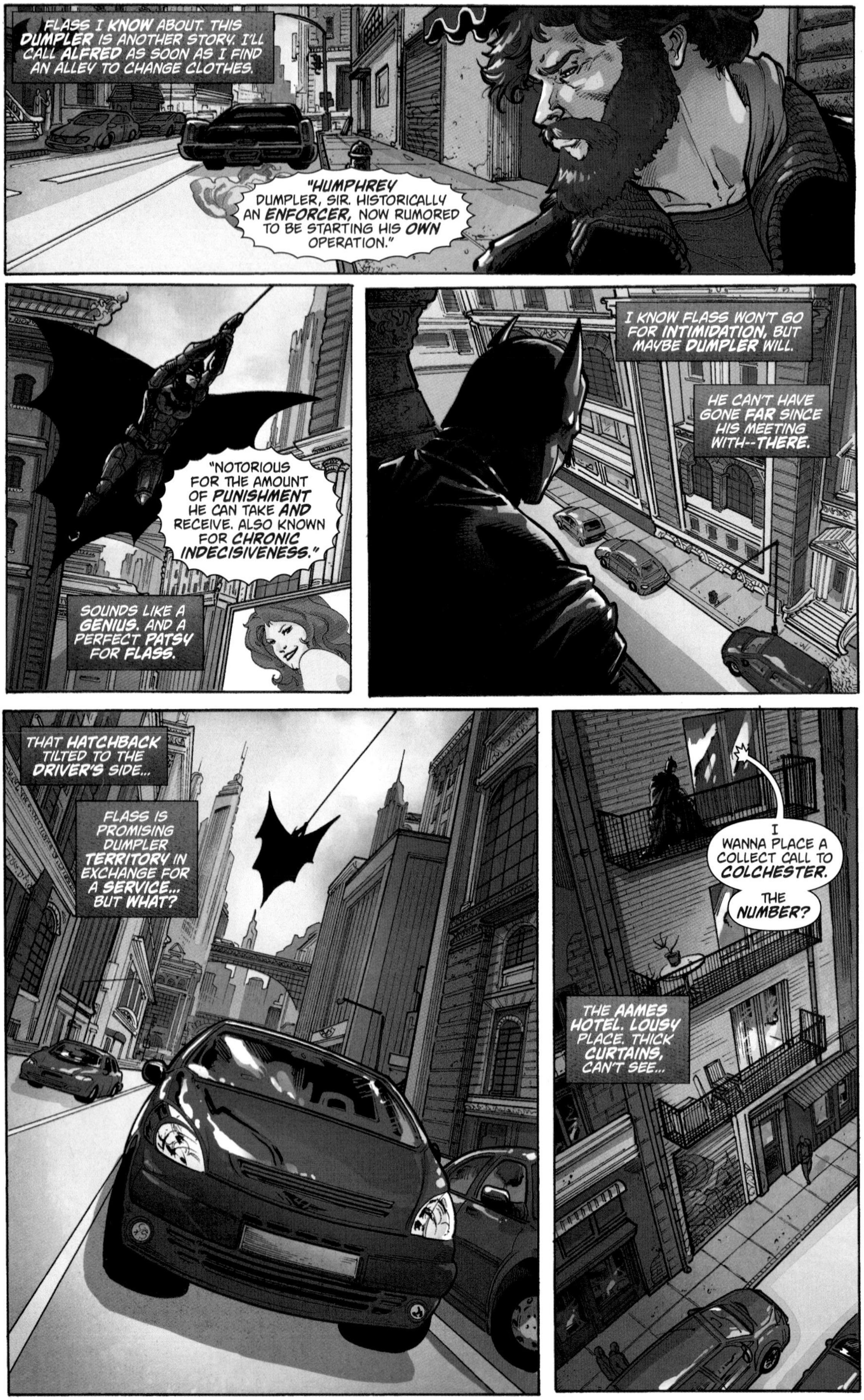
FLASS I KNOW ABOUT. THIS DUMPLER IS ANOTHER STORY. I'LL CALL ALFRED AS SOON AS I FIND AN ALLEY TO CHANGE CLOTHES.
"HUMPHREY DUMPLER, SIR. HISTORICALLY AN ENFORCER, NOW RUMORED TO BE STARTING HIS OWN OPERATION."
"NOTORIOUS FOR THE AMOUNT OF PUNISHMENT HE CAN TAKE AND RECEIVE. ALSO KNOWN FOR CHRONIC INDECISIVENESS."
SOUNDS LIKE A GENIUS. AND A PERFECT PATSY FOR FLASS.
I KNOW FLASS WON'T GO FOR INTIMIDATION, BUT MAYBE DUMPLER WILL.
HE CAN'T HAVE GONE FAR SINCE HIS MEETING WITH--THERE.
THAT HATCHBACK TILTED TO THE DRIVER'S SIDE...
FLASS IS PROMISING DUMPLER TERRITORY IN EXCHANGE FOR A SERVICE... BUT WHAT?
I WANNA PLACE A COLLECT CALL TO COLCHESTER.
THE NUMBER?
THE AAMES HOTEL. LOUSY PLACE. THICK CURTAINS, CAN'T SEE...

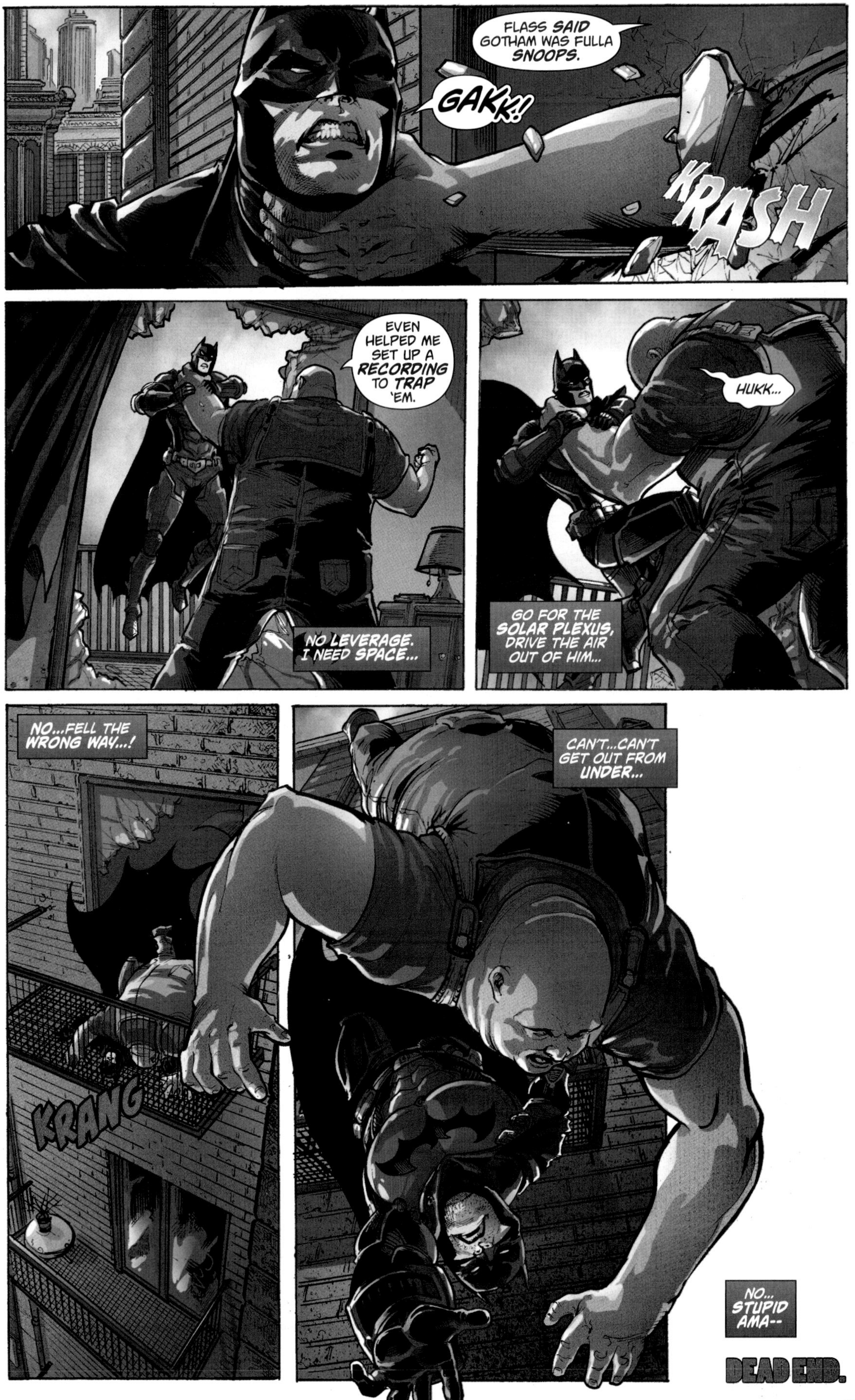
FLASS SAID GOTHAM WAS FULLA SNOOPS.
GAKK!
KRASH
EVEN HELPED ME SET UP A RECORDING TO TRAP 'EM.
NO LEVERAGE. I NEED SPACE...
HUKK...
GO FOR THE SOLAR PLEXUS, DRIVE THE AIR OUT OF HIM...
NO...FELL THE WRONG WAY...!
KRANG
CAN'T...CAN'T GET OUT FROM UNDER...
NO... STUPID AMA--
DEAD END.

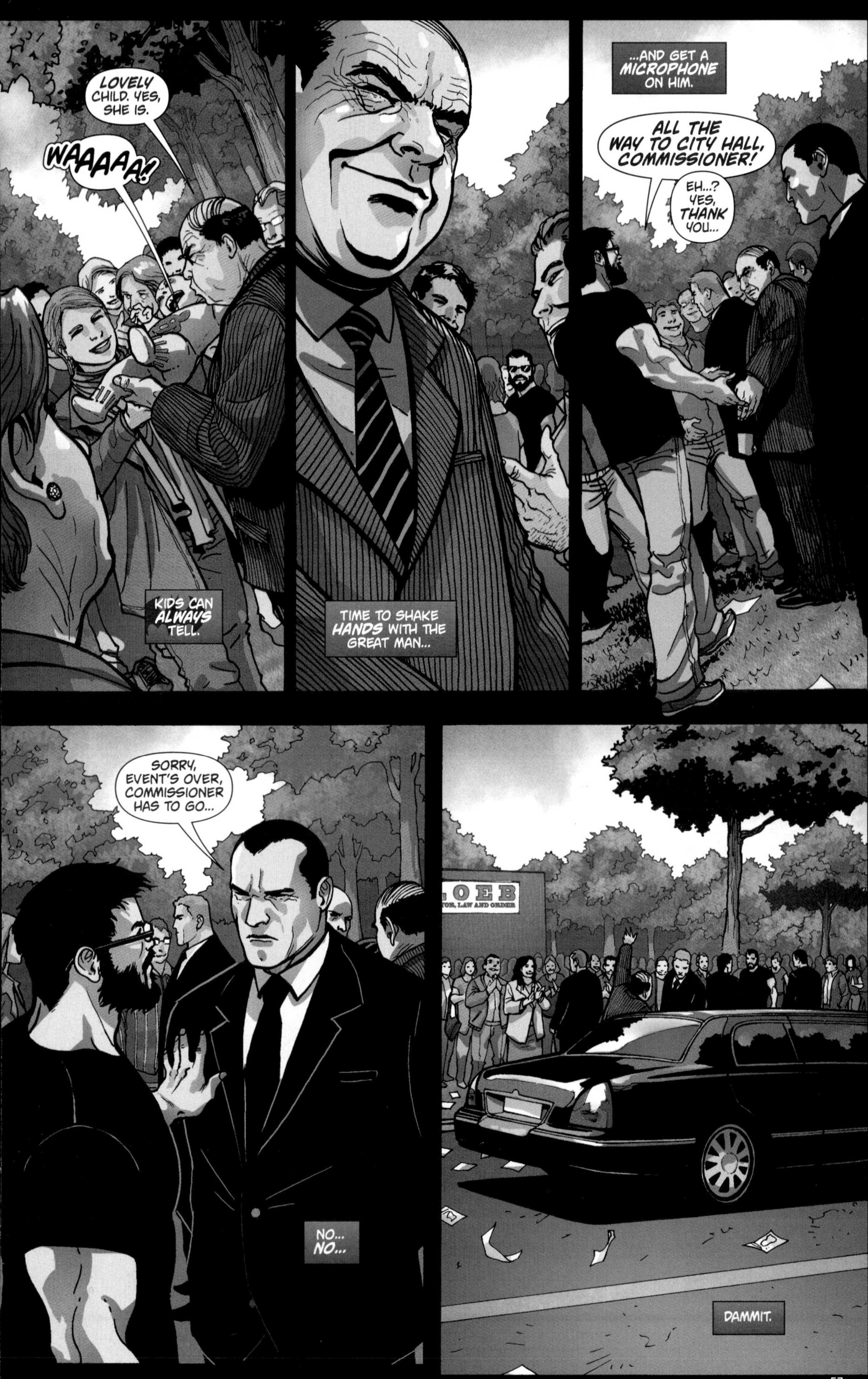
LOVELY CHILD. YES, SHE IS.
WAAAAA!
KIDS CAN ALWAYS TELL.
TIME TO SHAKE HANDS WITH THE GREAT MAN...
...AND GET A MICROPHONE ON HIM.
ALL THE WAY TO CITY HALL, COMMISSIONER!
EH...? YES, THANK YOU...
SORRY, EVENT'S OVER, COMMISSIONER HAS TO GO...
NO... NO...
LOEB
TOR, LAW AND ORDER
DAMMIT.

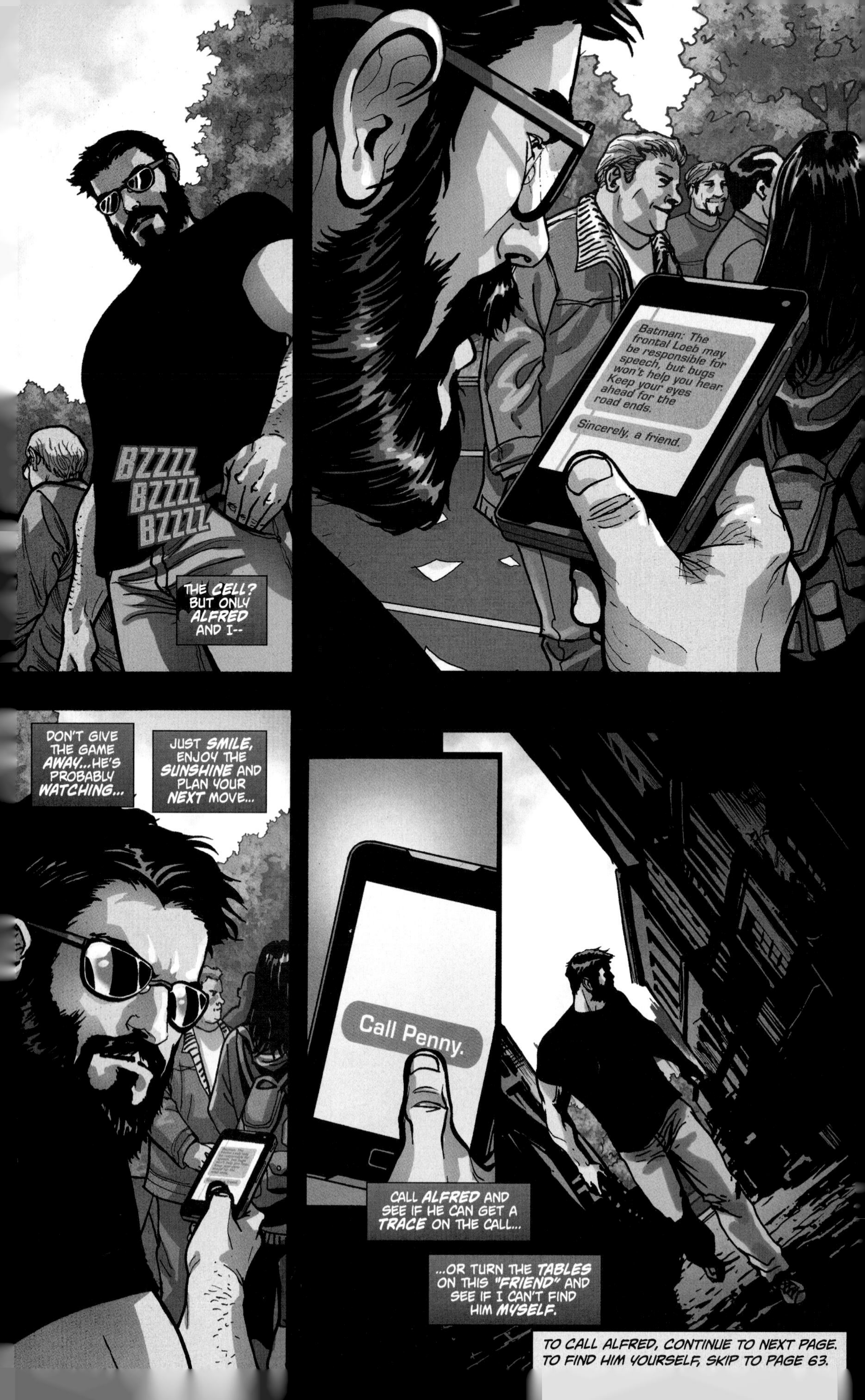
BZZZZZ
BZZZZZ
BZZZZZ
THE CELL? BUT ONLY ALFRED AND I--
Batman: The frontal Loeb may be responsible for speech, but bugs won't help you hear. Keep your eyes ahead for the road ends.
Sincerely, a friend.
DON'T GIVE THE GAME AWAY...HE'S PROBABLY WATCHING...
JUST SMILE, ENJOY THE SUNSHINE AND PLAN YOUR NEXT MOVE...
Call Penny.
CALL ALFRED AND SEE IF HE CAN GET A TRACE ON THE CALL...
...OR TURN THE TABLES ON THIS "FRIEND" AND SEE IF I CAN'T FIND HIM MYSELF.
TO CALL ALFRED, CONTINUE TO NEXT PAGE.
TO FIND HIM YOURSELF, SKIP TO PAGE 63.

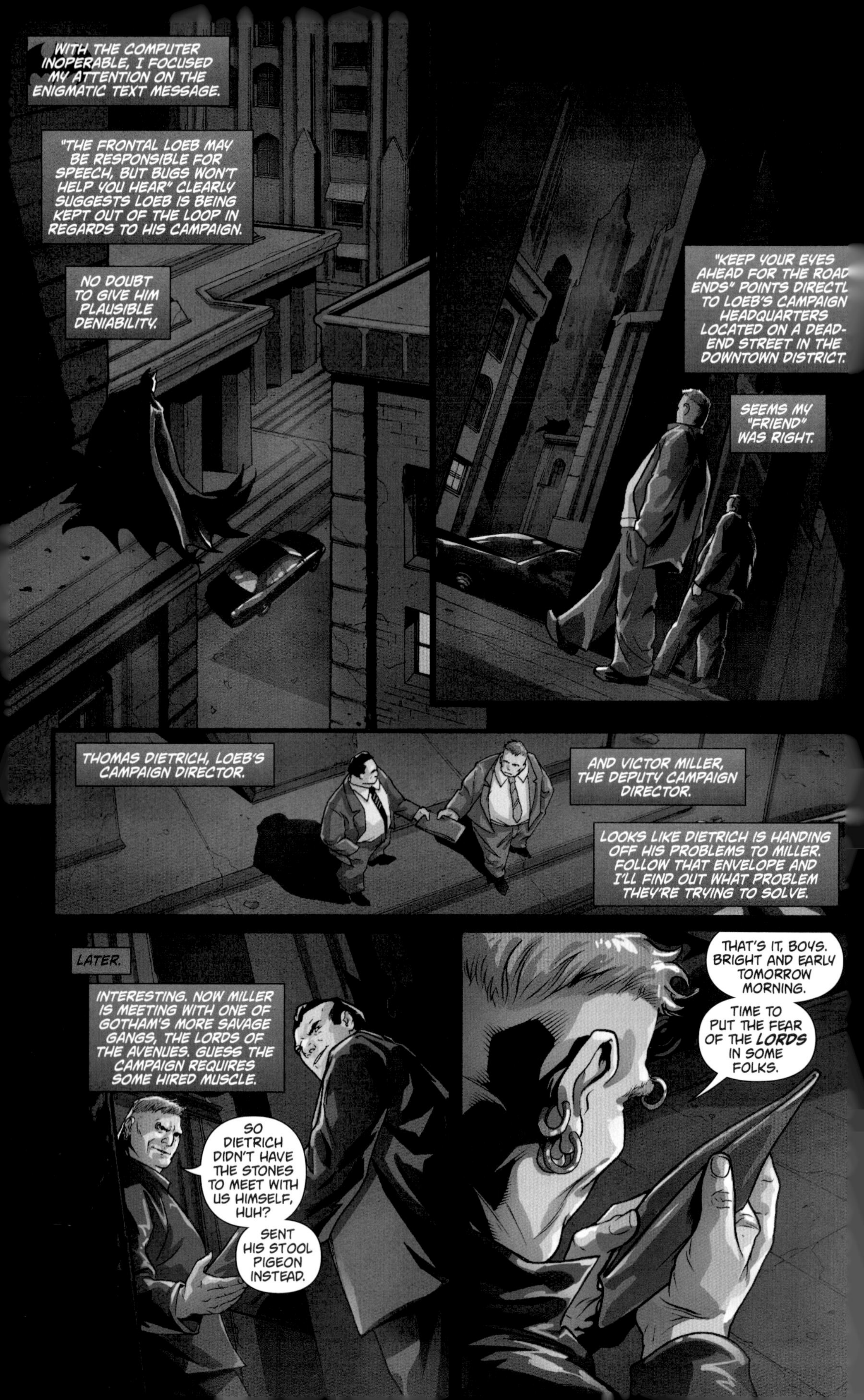
WITH THE COMPUTER INOPERABLE, I FOCUSED MY ATTENTION ON THE ENIGMATIC TEXT MESSAGE.
"THE FRONTAL LOEB MAY BE RESPONSIBLE FOR SPEECH, BUT BUGS WON'T HELP YOU HEAR" CLEARLY SUGGESTS LOEB IS BEING KEPT OUT OF THE LOOP IN REGARDS TO HIS CAMPAIGN.
NO DOUBT TO GIVE HIM PLAUSIBLE DENIABILITY.
"KEEP YOUR EYES AHEAD FOR THE ROAD ENDS" POINTS DIRECTL TO LOEB'S CAMPAIGN HEADQUARTERS LOCATED ON A DEAD-END STREET IN THE DOWNTOWN DISTRICT.
SEEMS MY "FRIEND" WAS RIGHT.
THOMAS DIETRICH, LOEB'S CAMPAIGN DIRECTOR.
AND VICTOR MILLER, THE DEPUTY CAMPAIGN DIRECTOR.
LOOKS LIKE DIETRICH IS HANDING OFF HIS PROBLEMS TO MILLER. FOLLOW THAT ENVELOPE AND I'LL FIND OUT WHAT PROBLEM THEY'RE TRYING TO SOLVE.
LATER.
INTERESTING. NOW MILLER IS MEETING WITH ONE OF GOTHAM'S MORE SAVAGE GANGS, THE LORDS OF THE AVENUES. GUESS THE CAMPAIGN REQUIRES SOME HIRED MUSCLE.
SO DIETRICH DIDN'T HAVE THE STONES TO MEET WITH US HIMSELF, HUH?
SENT HIS STOOL PIGEON INSTEAD.
THAT'S IT, BOYS. BRIGHT AND EARLY TOMORROW MORNING.
TIME TO PUT THE FEAR OF THE LORDS IN SOME FOLKS.

I'VE HAD MY OWN RUN-INS WITH THE LORDS BEFORE, SO I'VE BEEN KEEPING AN EYE ON THEIR ACTIVITIES FOR MONTHS NOW.

THIS IS A BIG MOVE FOR THEM. THEY'RE UPPING THEIR GAME.

THE LORDS ARE INEXPERIENCED AT THE CLOAK AND DAGGER GAME.

THEY SHOULD STICK TO WHAT THEY KNOW.

SSSSSSSSSSS

THE WEAPONS ARE NOTHING OUT OF THE ORDINARY...

...BUT A DESK COVERED WITH DOCUMENTS AND SPREADSHEETS SEEMS A LITTLE OUT OF PLACE FOR A GANG OF SEWER RATS.

ALL IN DISTRICTS KNOWN TO FAVOR LOEB'S MAYORAL OPPONENT. LOEB'S CAMPAIGN IS PAYING OFF THE LORDS TO INTIMIDATE HIS FOE'S SUPPORTERS.

LISTS OF RALLY SITES AND VOTER REGISTRATION STATIONS.

SSSSSSS

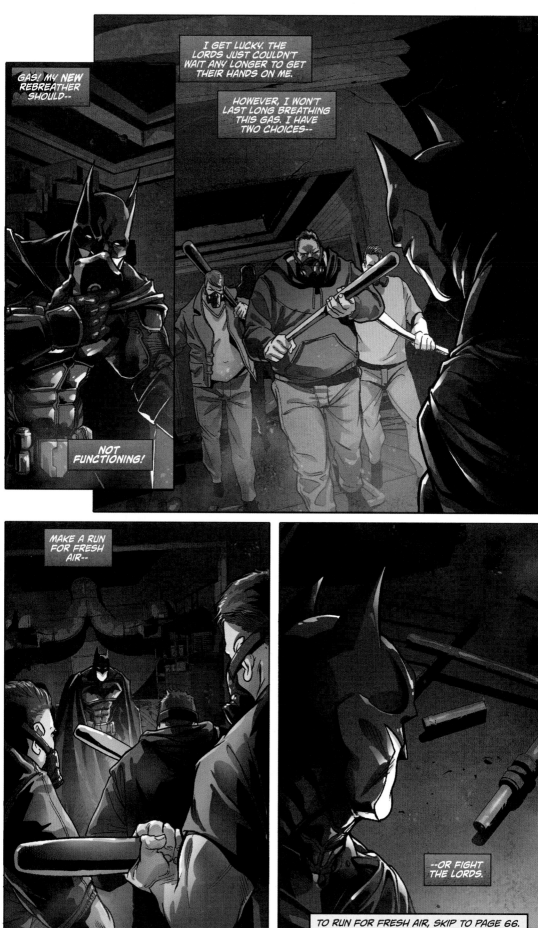

GAS! MY NEW REBREATHER SHOULD--

NOT FUNCTIONING!

I GET LUCKY. THE LORDS JUST COULDN'T WAIT ANY LONGER TO GET THEIR HANDS ON ME.

HOWEVER, I WON'T LAST LONG BREATHING THIS GAS. I HAVE TWO CHOICES--

MAKE A RUN FOR FRESH AIR--

--OR FIGHT THE LORDS.

TO RUN FOR FRESH AIR, SKIP TO PAGE 66.
TO FIGHT THE LORDS, SKIP TO PAGE 69.

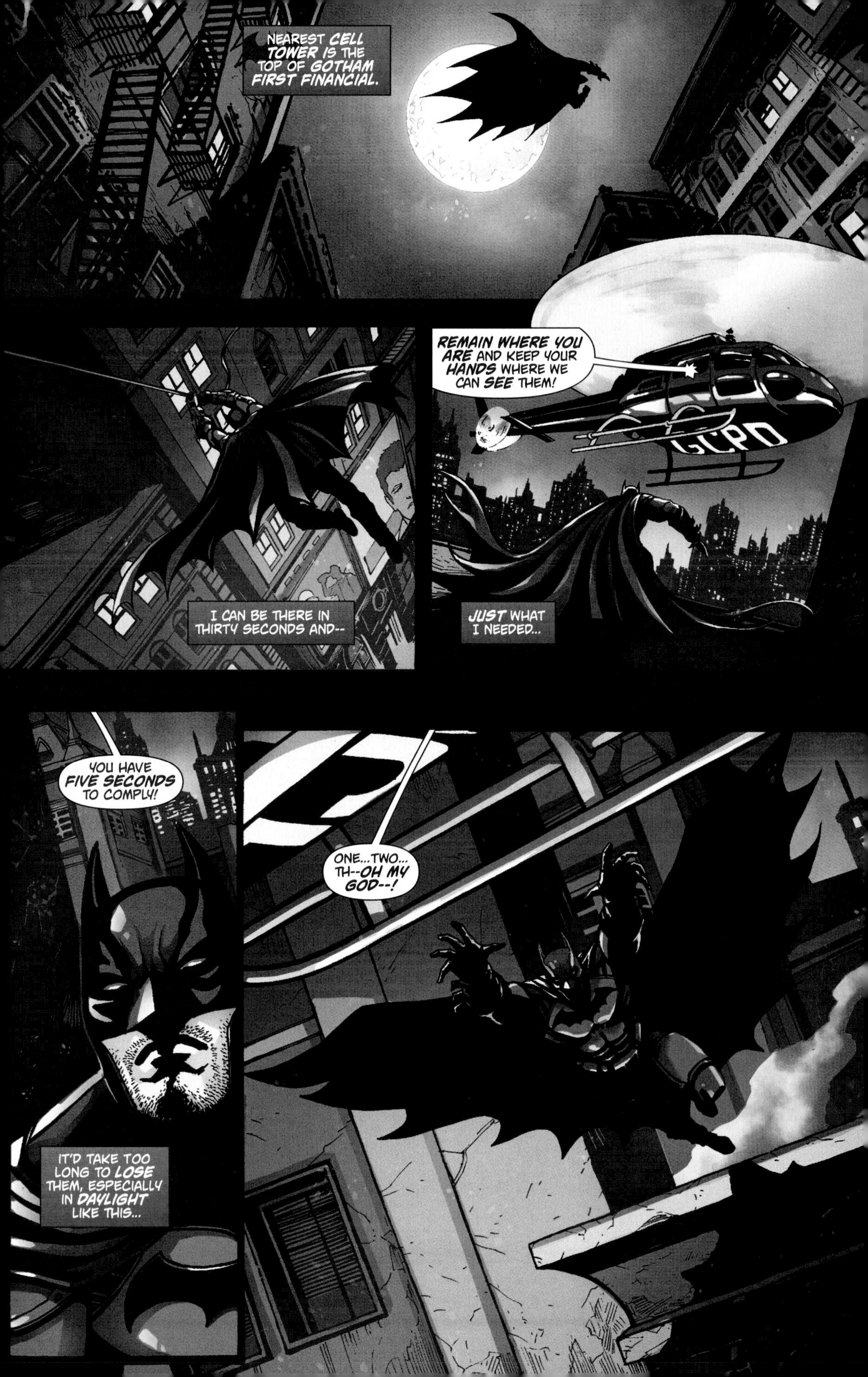
NEAREST CELL TOWER IS THE TOP OF GOTHAM FIRST FINANCIAL.
I CAN BE THERE IN THIRTY SECONDS AND--
REMAIN WHERE YOU ARE AND KEEP YOUR HANDS WHERE WE CAN SEE THEM!
GCPD
JUST WHAT I NEEDED...
YOU HAVE FIVE SECONDS TO COMPLY!
IT'D TAKE TOO LONG TO LOSE THEM, ESPECIALLY IN DAYLIGHT LIKE THIS...
ONE...TWO... TH--OH MY GOD--!

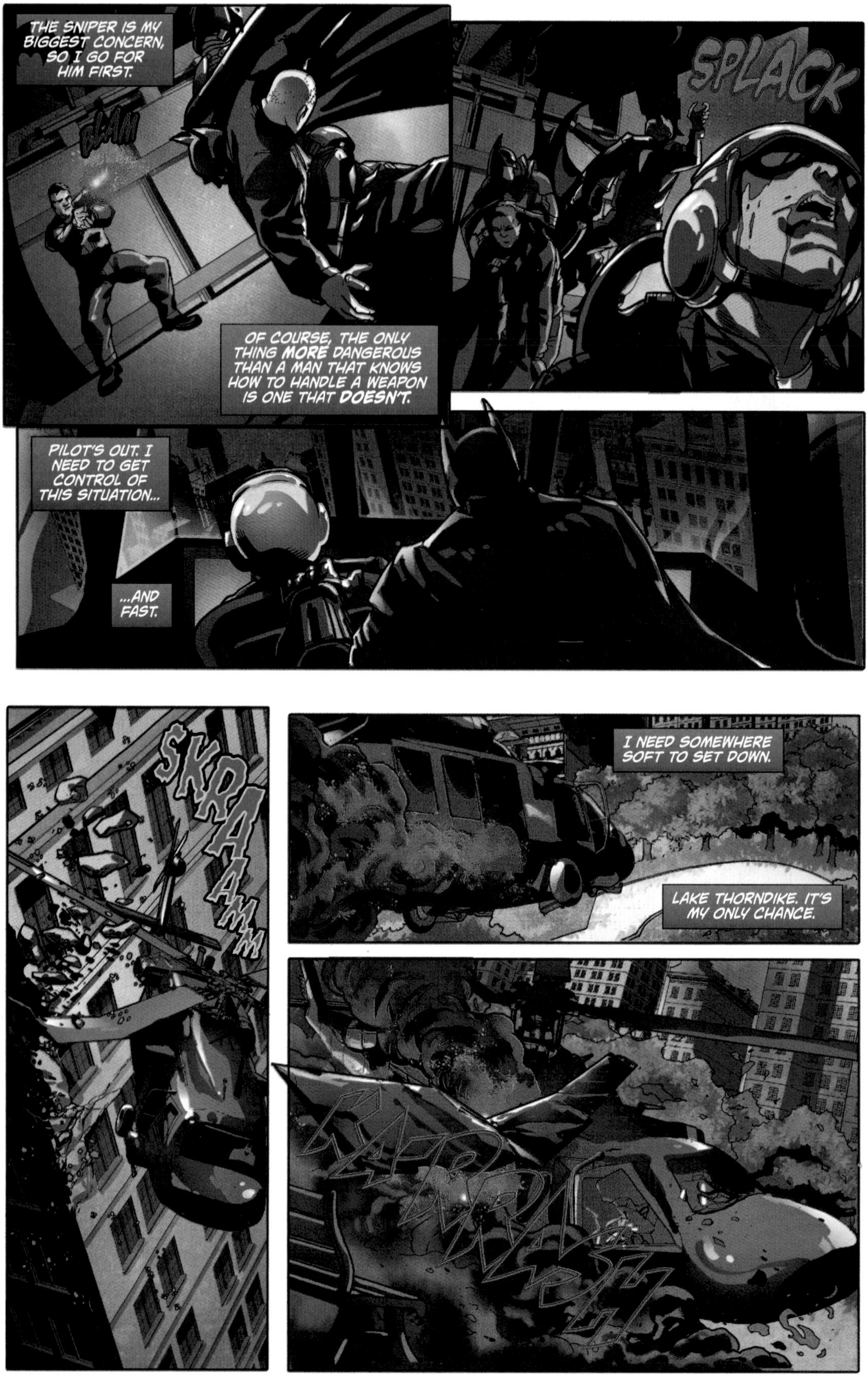
THE SNIPER IS MY BIGGEST CONCERN, SO I GO FOR HIM FIRST.
BLAM
OF COURSE, THE ONLY THING MORE DANGEROUS THAN A MAN THAT KNOWS HOW TO HANDLE A WEAPON IS ONE THAT DOESN'T.
SPLACK
PILOT'S OUT. I NEED TO GET CONTROL OF THIS SITUATION...
...AND FAST.
SKRAAAMM
I NEED SOMEWHERE SOFT TO SET DOWN.
LAKE THORNDIKE. IT'S MY ONLY CHANCE.

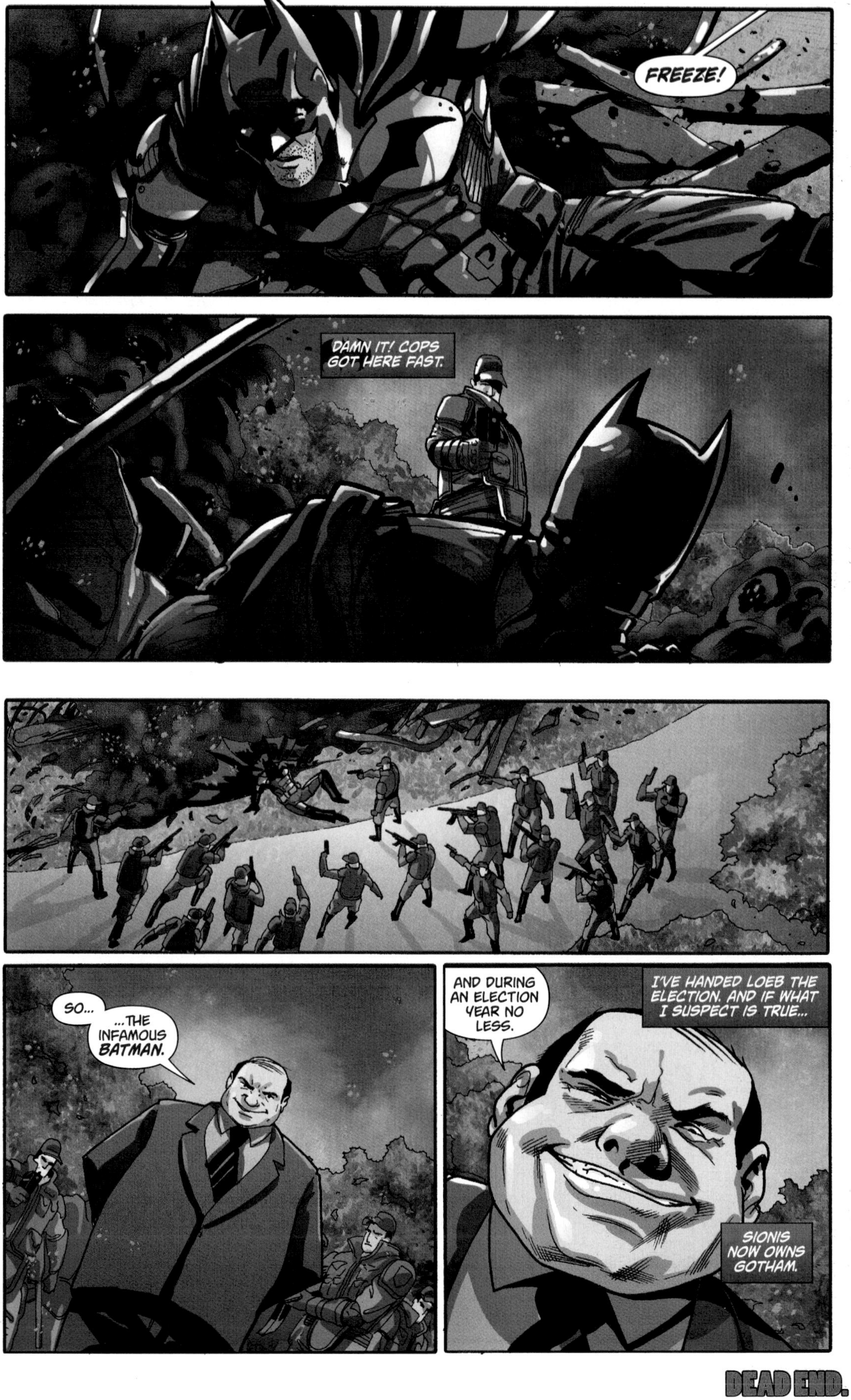
FREEZE!
DAMN IT! COPS GOT HERE FAST.
SO...
...THE INFAMOUS BATMAN.
AND DURING AN ELECTION YEAR NO LESS.
I'VE HANDED LOEB THE ELECTION. AND IF WHAT I SUSPECT IS TRUE...
SIONIS NOW OWNS GOTHAM.
DEAD END.

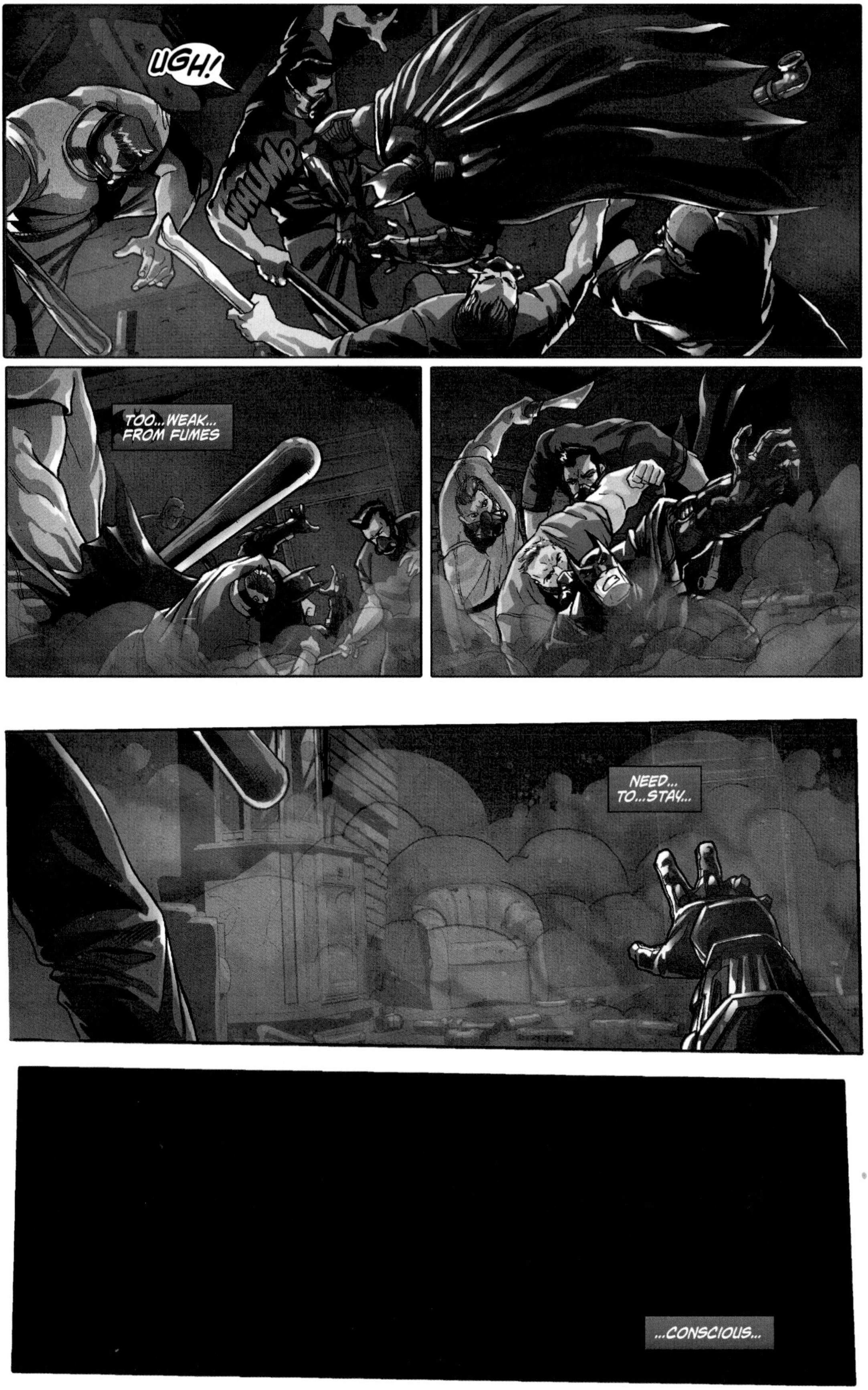
UGH!
WHUMP
TOO...WEAK...
FROM FUMES
NEED...
TO...STAY...
...CONSCIOUS...

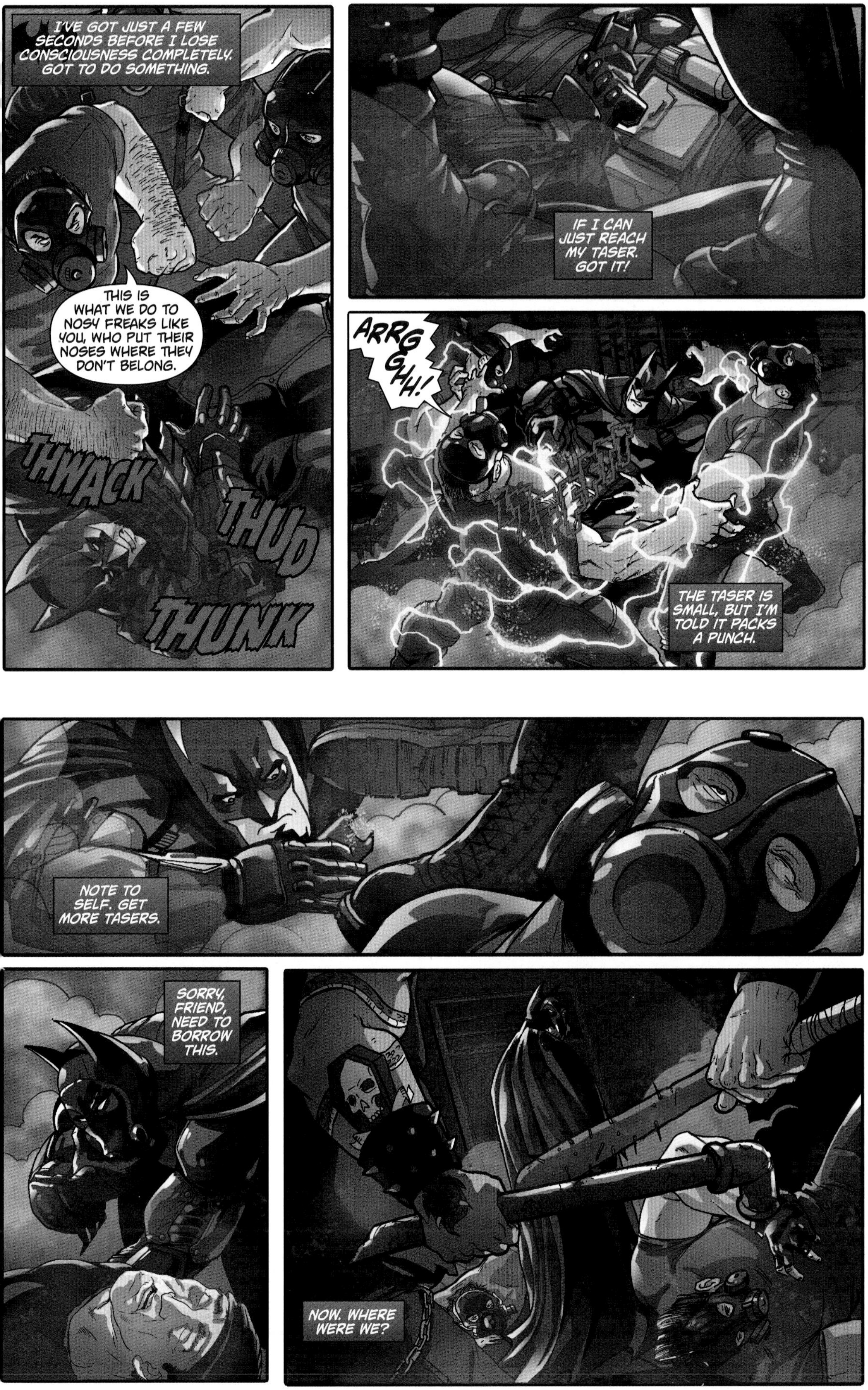
I'VE GOT JUST A FEW SECONDS BEFORE I LOSE CONSCIOUSNESS COMPLETELY. GOT TO DO SOMETHING.
THIS IS WHAT WE DO TO NOSY FREAKS LIKE YOU, WHO PUT THEIR NOSES WHERE THEY DON'T BELONG.
THWACK
THUD
THUNK
IF I CAN JUST REACH MY TASER. GOT IT!
ARRGGHH!
THE TASER IS SMALL, BUT I'M TOLD IT PACKS A PUNCH.
NOTE TO SELF. GET MORE TASERS.
SORRY, FRIEND, NEED TO BORROW THIS.
NOW. WHERE WERE WE?

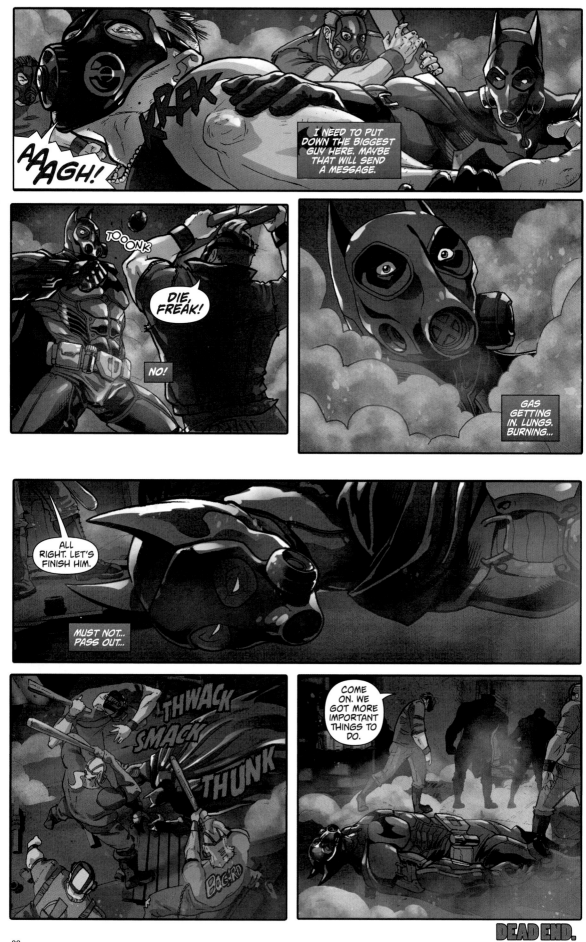

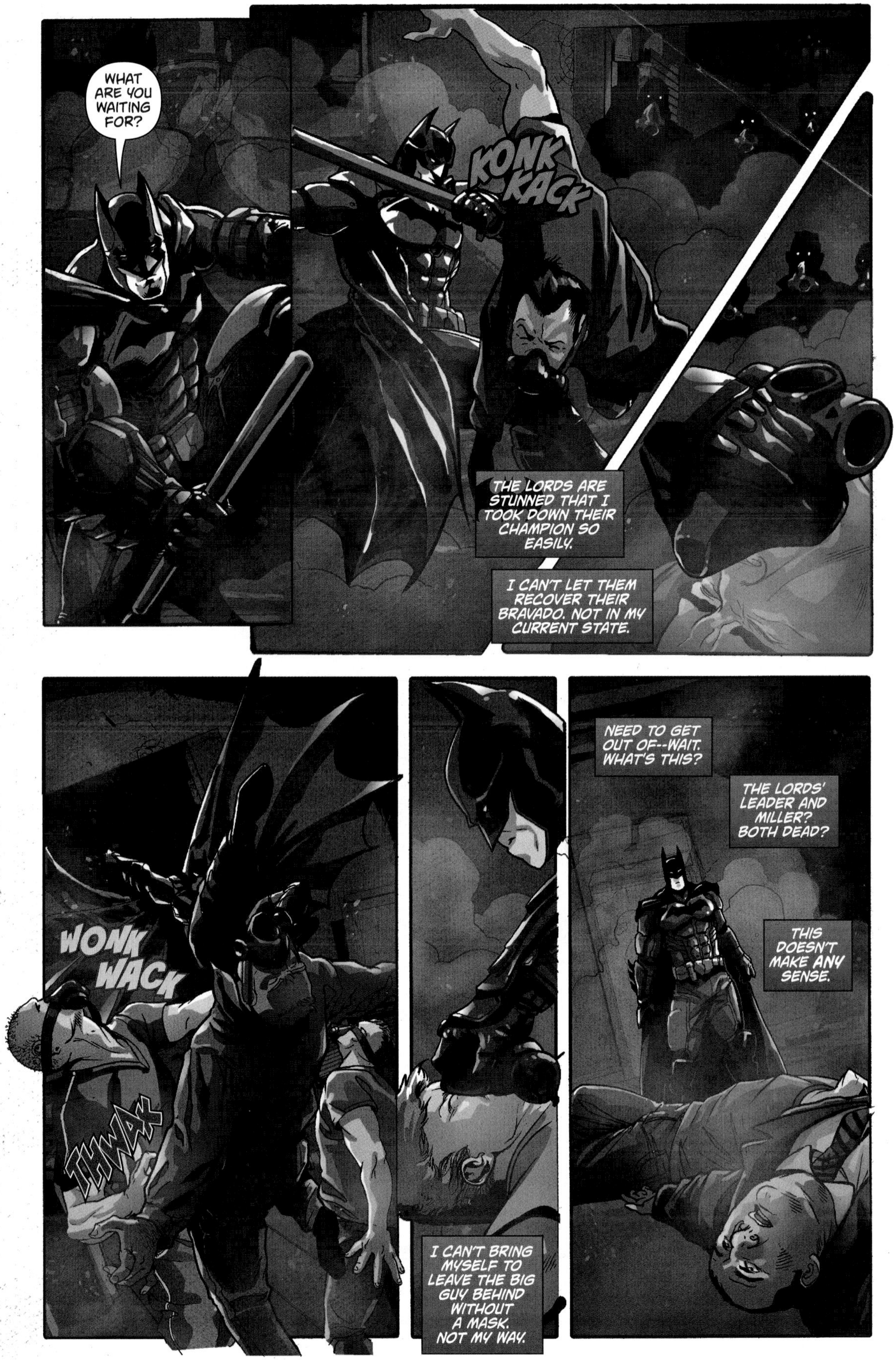
WHAT ARE YOU WAITING FOR?
KONK
KACK
THE LORDS ARE STUNNED THAT I TOOK DOWN THEIR CHAMPION SO EASILY.
I CAN'T LET THEM RECOVER THEIR BRAVADO. NOT IN MY CURRENT STATE.
WONK
WACK
THWAK
I CAN'T BRING MYSELF TO LEAVE THE BIG GUY BEHIND WITHOUT A MASK. NOT MY WAY.
NEED TO GET OUT OF--WAIT. WHAT'S THIS?
THE LORDS' LEADER AND MILLER? BOTH DEAD?
THIS DOESN'T MAKE ANY SENSE.

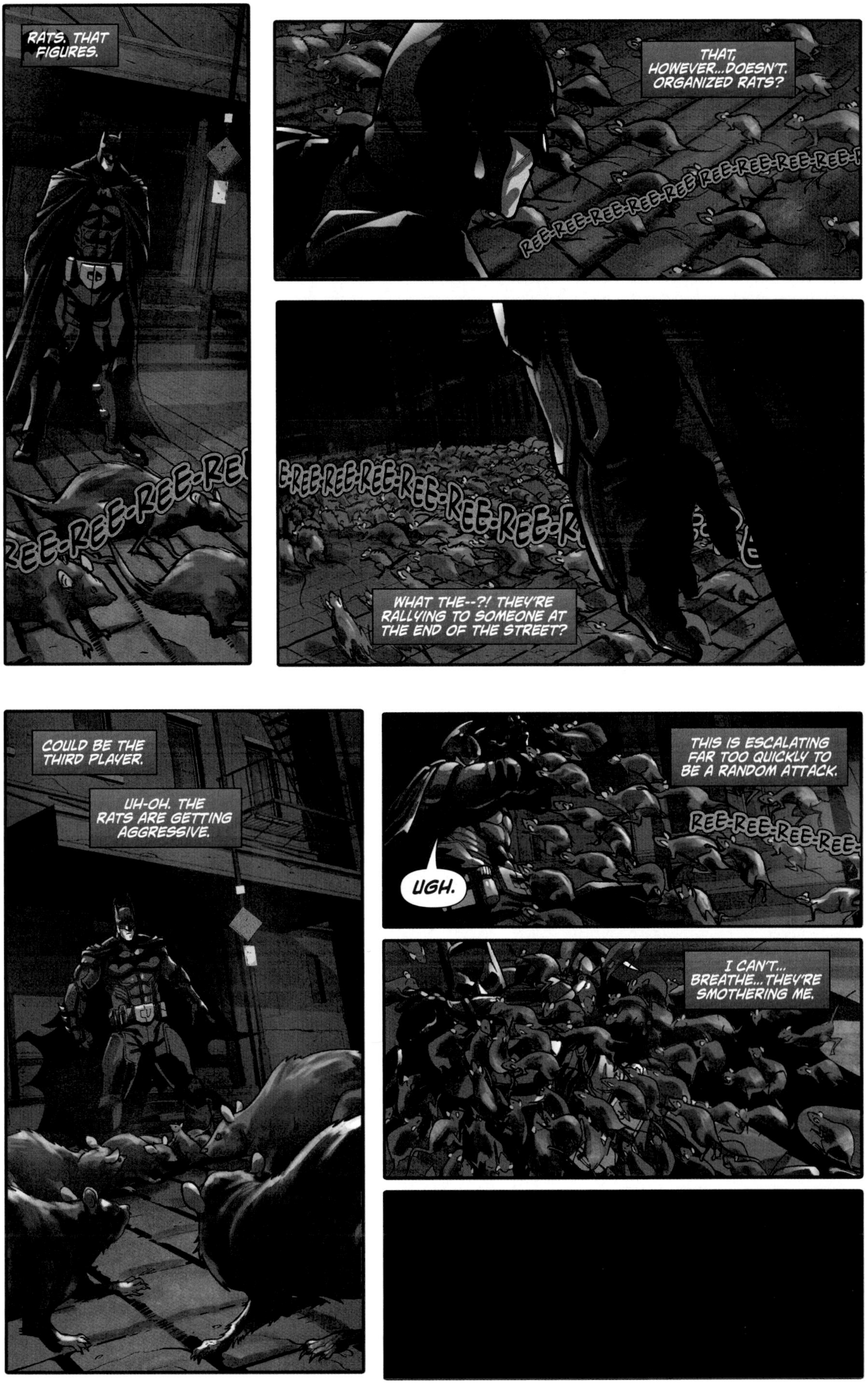
RATS. THAT FIGURES.
REE-REE-REE-RE
THAT, HOWEVER...DOESN'T. ORGANIZED RATS?
REE-REE-REE-REE-REE-REE-REE-REE-REE-REE-
REE-REE-REE-REE-REE-REE-REE-
WHAT THE--?! THEY'RE RALLYING TO SOMEONE AT THE END OF THE STREET?
COULD BE THE THIRD PLAYER.
UH-OH. THE RATS ARE GETTING AGGRESSIVE.
THIS IS ESCALATING FAR TOO QUICKLY TO BE A RANDOM ATTACK.
REE-REE-REE-REE-
UGH.
I CAN'T... BREATHE... THEY'RE SMOTHERING ME.

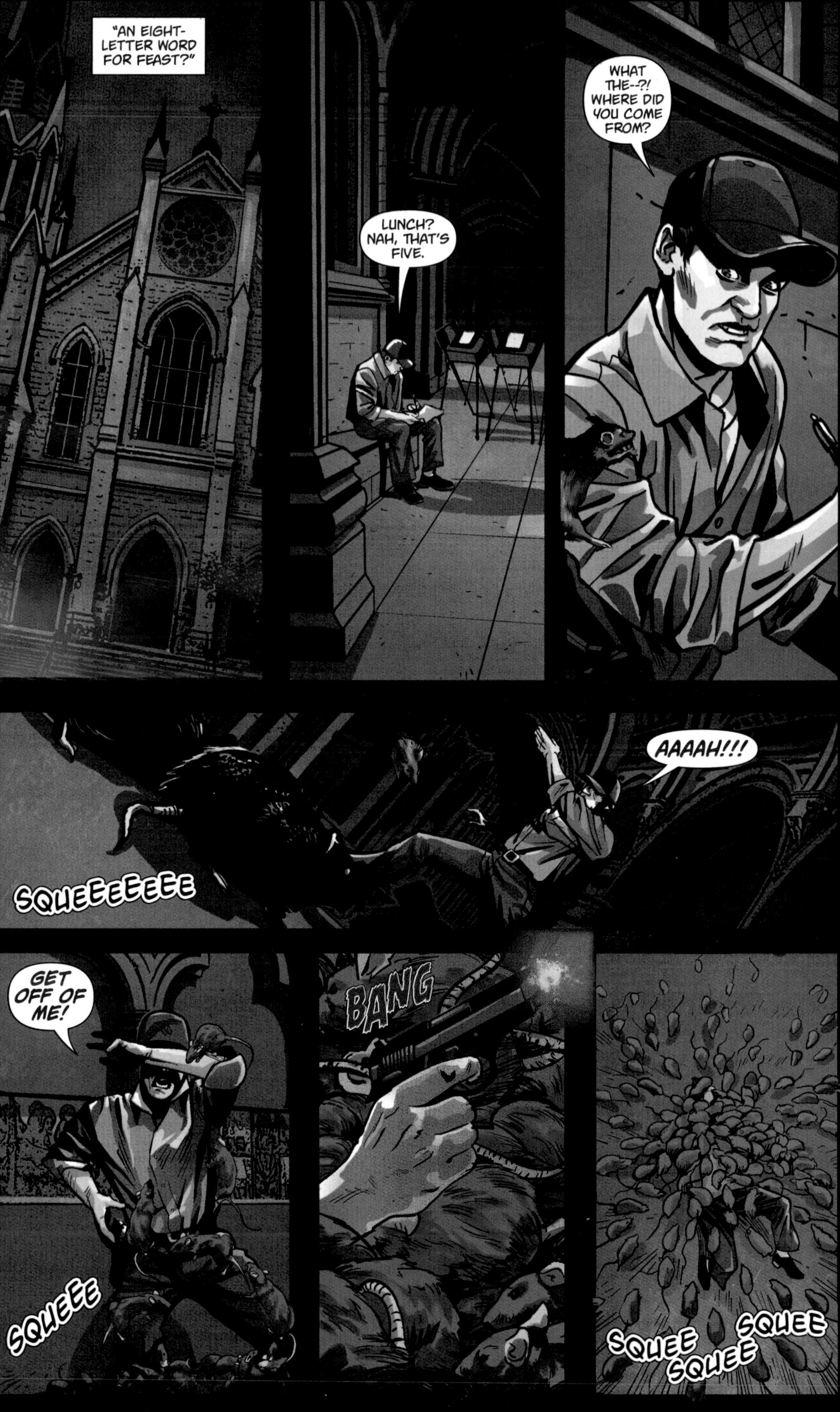
"AN EIGHT-LETTER WORD FOR FEAST?"
LUNCH? NAH, THAT'S FIVE.
WHAT THE--?! WHERE DID YOU COME FROM?
AAAAH!!!
SQUEEEEEEEE
GET OFF OF ME!
SQUEEE
BANG
SQUEE
SQUEE
SQUEE

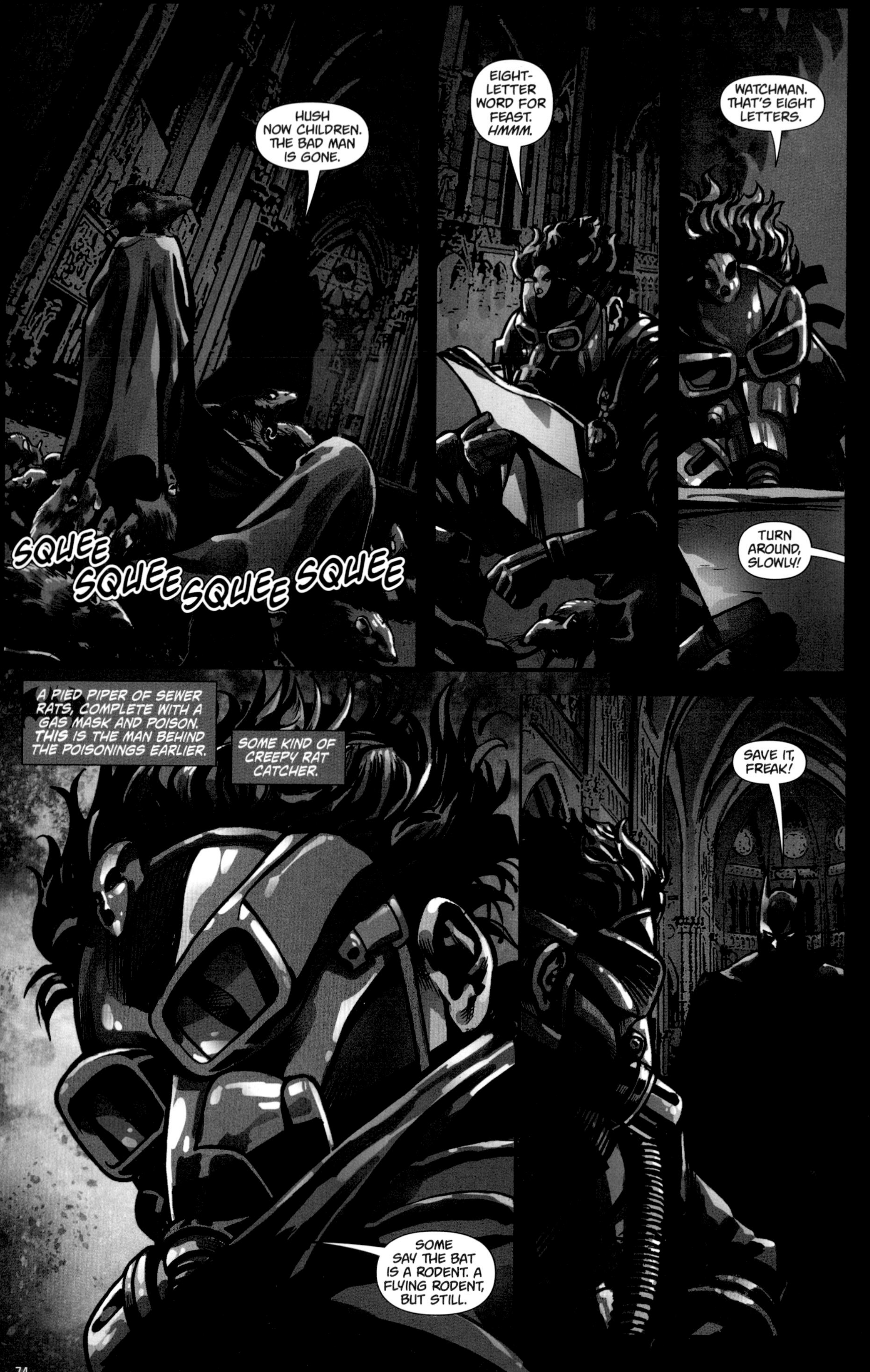
HUSH NOW CHILDREN. THE BAD MAN IS GONE.
SQUEE SQUEE SQUEE SQUEE
EIGHT-LETTER WORD FOR FEAST. HMMM.
WATCHMAN. THAT'S EIGHT LETTERS.
TURN AROUND, SLOWLY!
A PIED PIPER OF SEWER RATS, COMPLETE WITH A GAS MASK AND POISON. THIS IS THE MAN BEHIND THE POISONINGS EARLIER.
SOME KIND OF CREEPY RAT CATCHER.
SOME SAY THE BAT IS A RODENT. A FLYING RODENT, BUT STILL.
SAVE IT, FREAK!

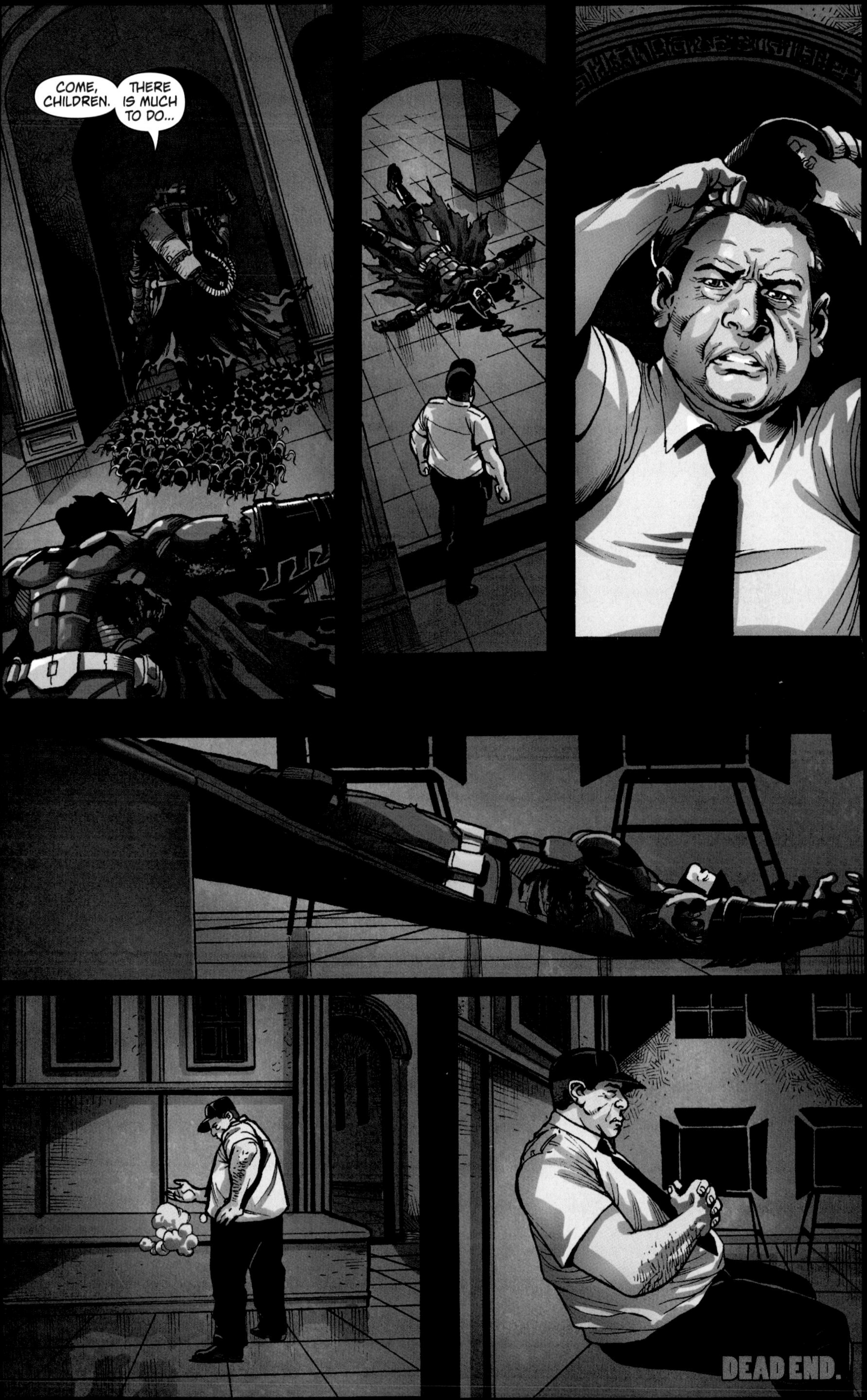
COME, CHILDREN.
THERE IS MUCH TO DO...
DEAD END.

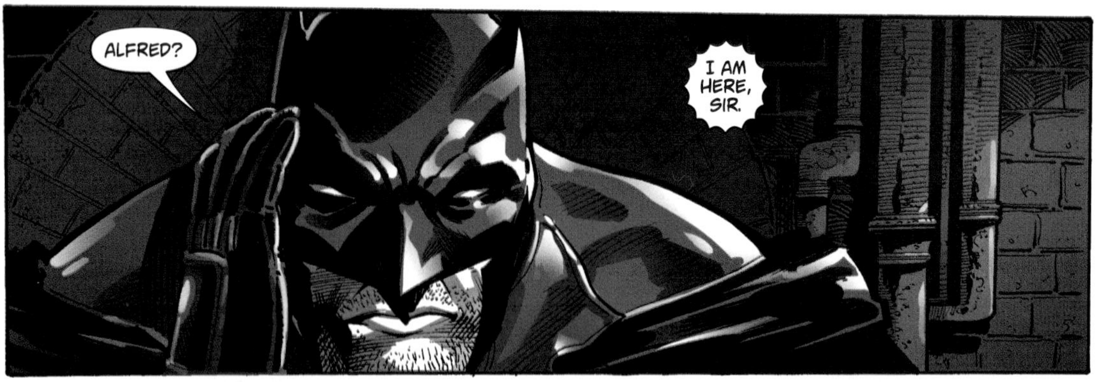
ALFRED?
I AM HERE, SIR.
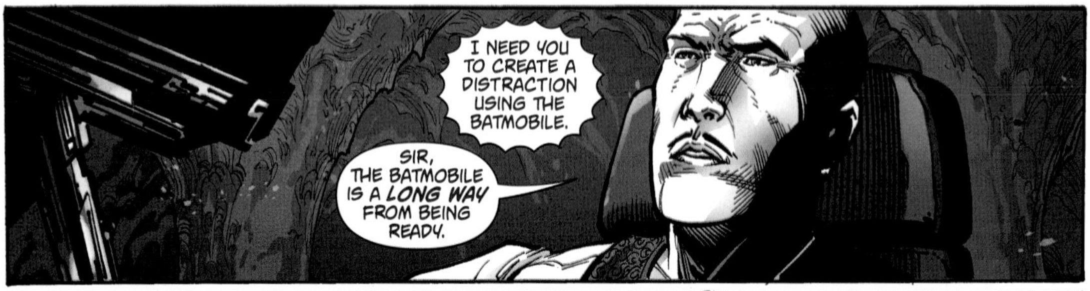
I NEED YOU TO CREATE A DISTRACTION USING THE BATMOBILE.
SIR, THE BATMOBILE IS A *LONG WAY* FROM BEING READY.
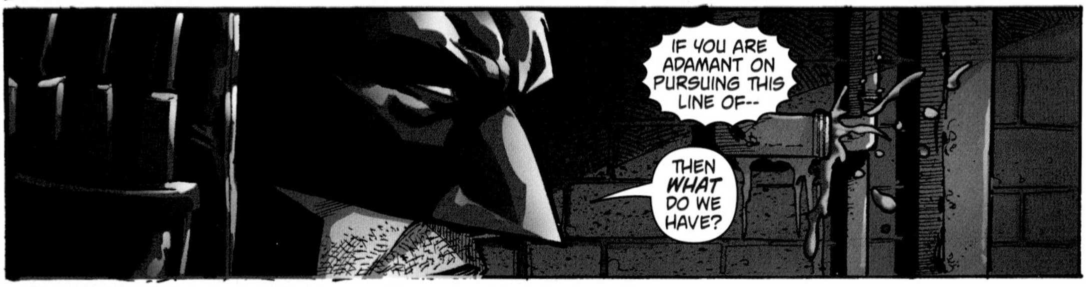
IF YOU ARE ADAMANT ON PURSUING THIS LINE OF--
THEN *WHAT* DO WE HAVE?
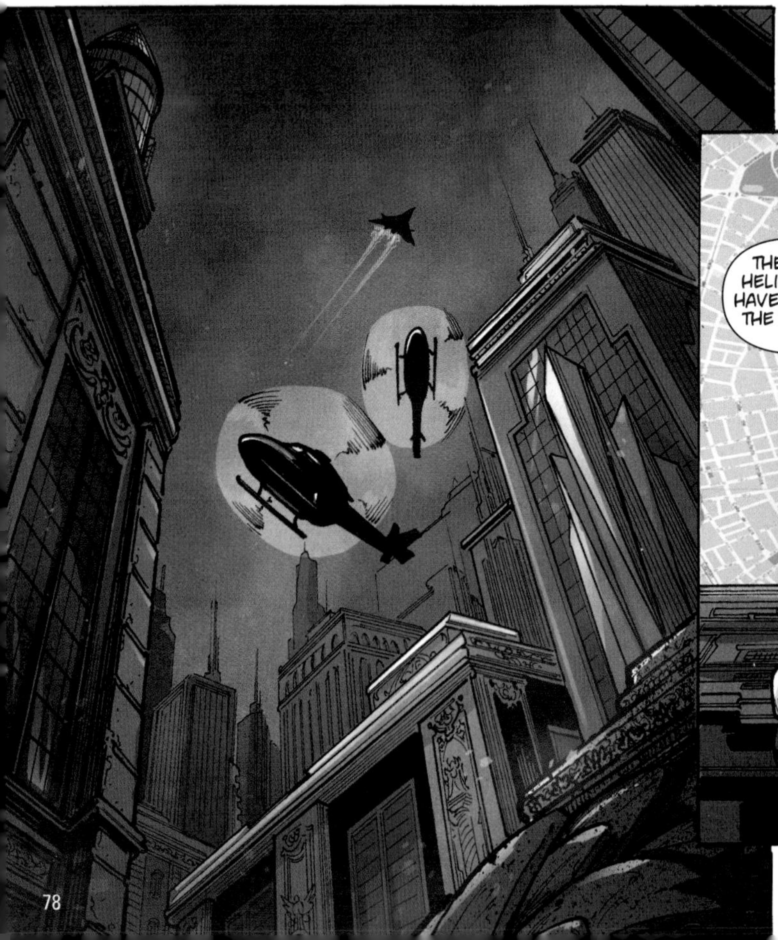
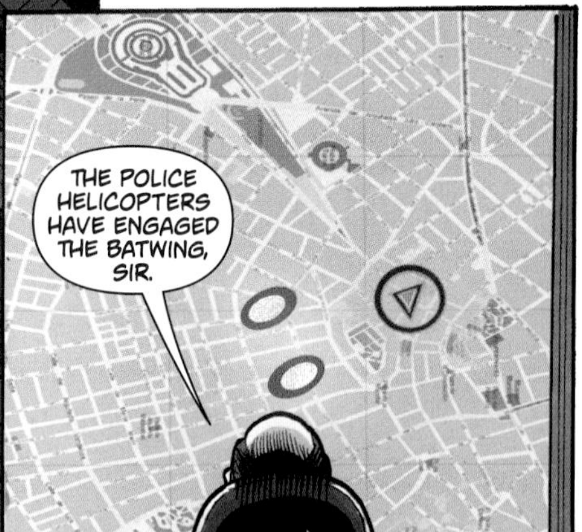
THE POLICE HELICOPTERS HAVE ENGAGED THE BATWING, SIR.

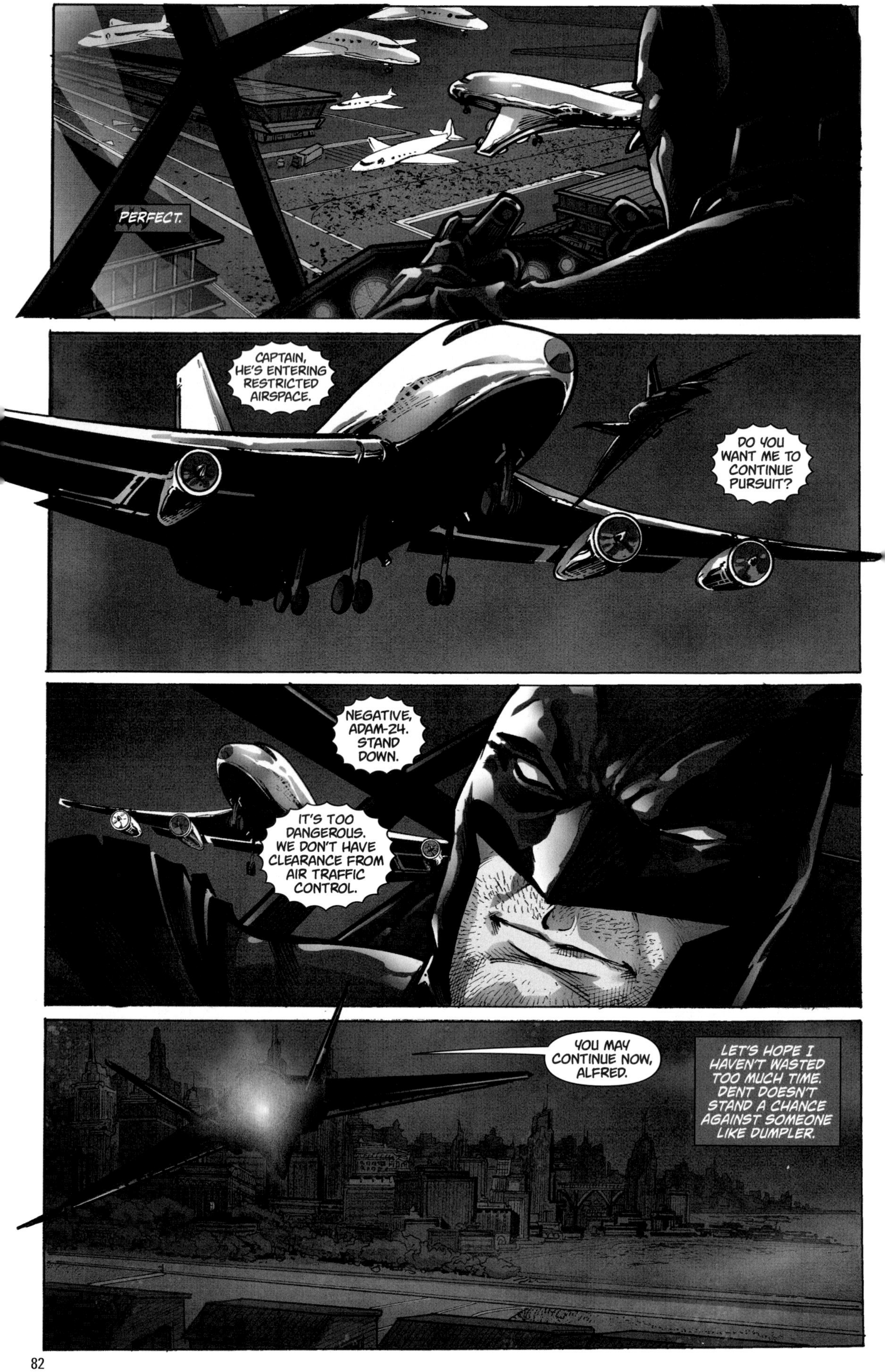
PERFECT.
CAPTAIN, HE'S ENTERING RESTRICTED AIRSPACE.
DO YOU WANT ME TO CONTINUE PURSUIT?
NEGATIVE, ADAM-24. STAND DOWN.
IT'S TOO DANGEROUS. WE DON'T HAVE CLEARANCE FROM AIR TRAFFIC CONTROL.
YOU MAY CONTINUE NOW, ALFRED.
LET'S HOPE I HAVEN'T WASTED TOO MUCH TIME. DENT DOESN'T STAND A CHANCE AGAINST SOMEONE LIKE DUMPLER.

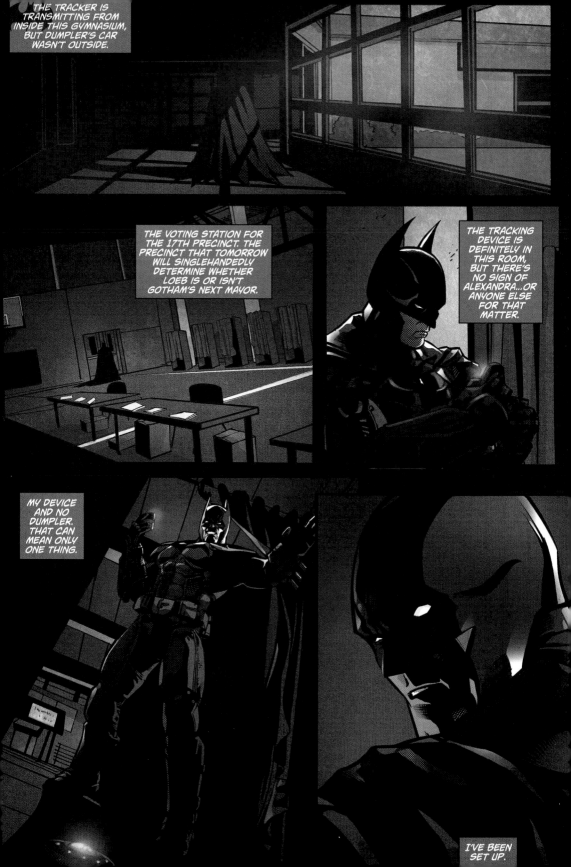

...BRING DENT'S SISTER TO WARRANT HILL.

BLACK MASK.

IT'S ALL ABOUT TO GO DOWN THERE.

AT DAWN, WE WON'T NEED HER ANYMORE.

YOU CAN JUST THROW HER BODY ON THE PILE.

ALFRED!?

I'M HERE, SIR.

FLASS IS MAKING A CALL ON HIS CELL PHONE AS WE SPEAK. I NEED TO HEAR THAT CONVERSATION.

ONE MOMENT, SIR.

I DON'T HAVE MUCH TIME. I COULD EITHER GO AFTER FLASS RIGHT THIS SECOND...

...OR STOP BY THE BATCAVE FOR MORE FIREPOWER BEFORE GOING TO WARRANT HILL AND STOPPING WHATEVER BLACK MASK HAS PLANNED.

TO GO AFTER FLASS, SKIP TO PAGE 140.

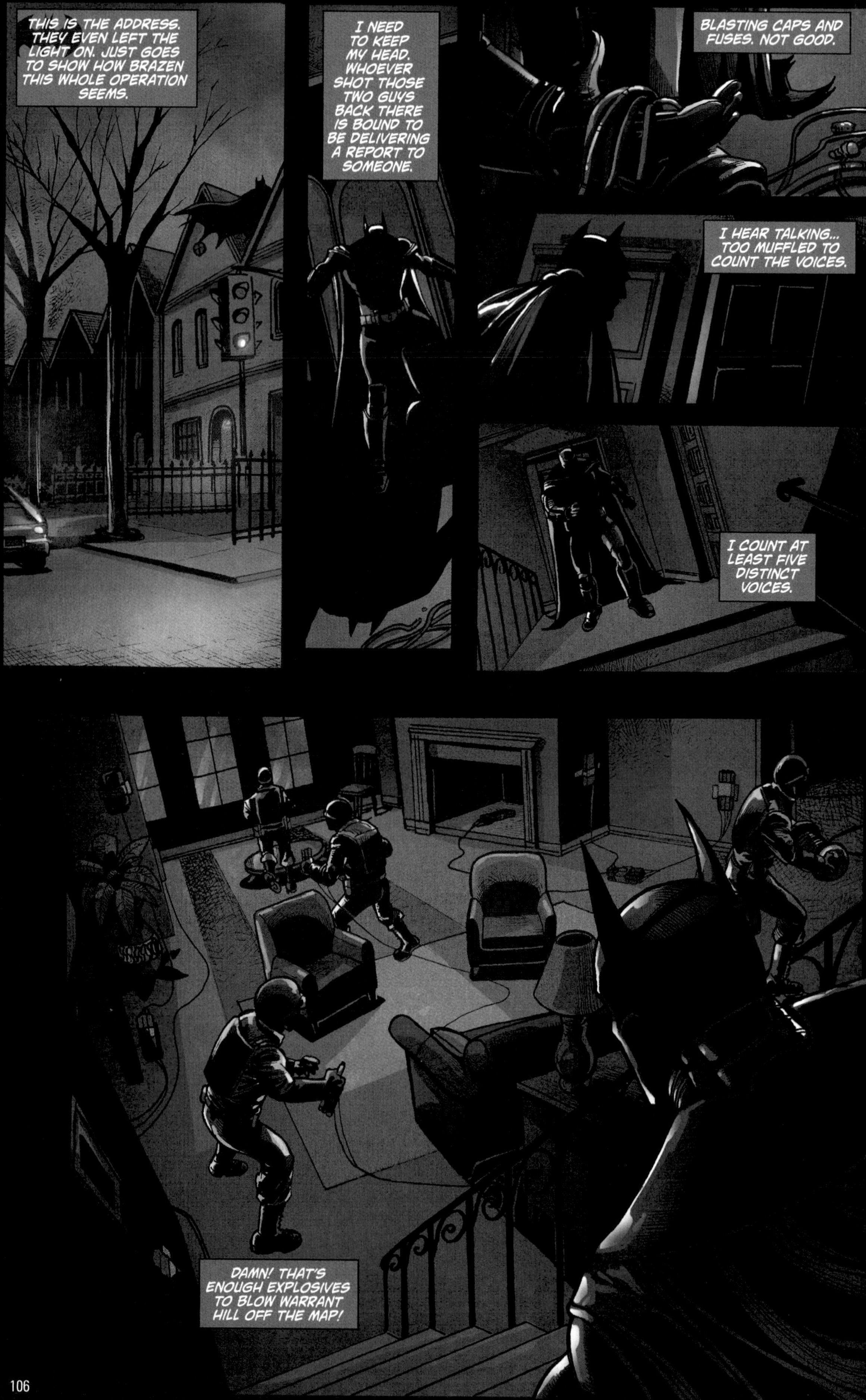
THIS IS THE ADDRESS. THEY EVEN LEFT THE LIGHT ON. JUST GOES TO SHOW HOW BRAZEN THIS WHOLE OPERATION SEEMS.
I NEED TO KEEP MY HEAD. WHOEVER SHOT THOSE TWO GUYS BACK THERE IS BOUND TO BE DELIVERING A REPORT TO SOMEONE.
BLASTING CAPS AND FUSES. NOT GOOD.
I HEAR TALKING... TOO MUFFLED TO COUNT THE VOICES.
I COUNT AT LEAST FIVE DISTINCT VOICES.
DAMN! THAT'S ENOUGH EXPLOSIVES TO BLOW WARRANT HILL OFF THE MAP!

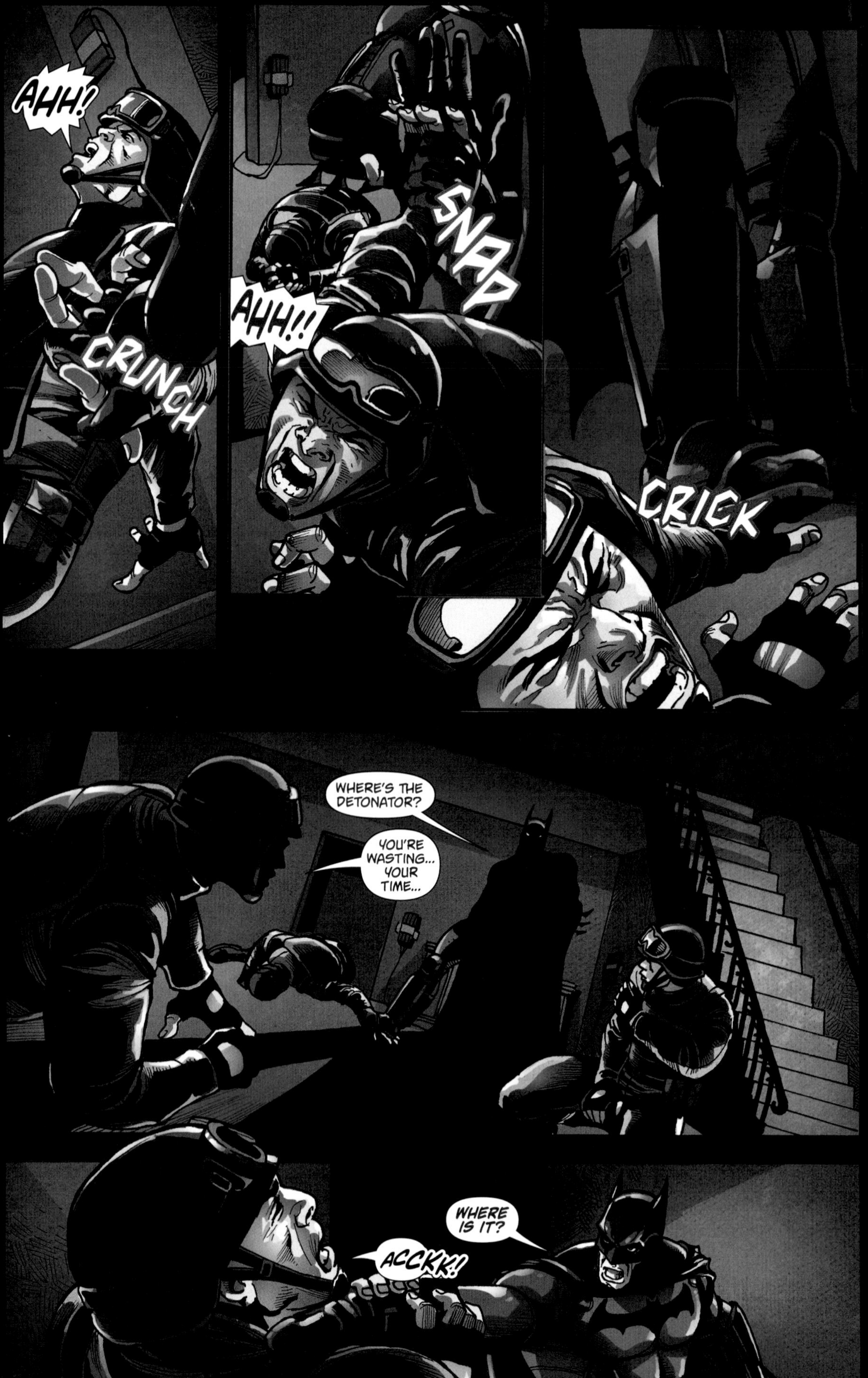
AHH!
CRUNCH
AHH!!
SNAP
CRICK
WHERE'S THE DETONATOR?
YOU'RE WASTING... YOUR TIME...
WHERE IS IT?
ACCKK!

111

GO BACK TO PAGE 88.

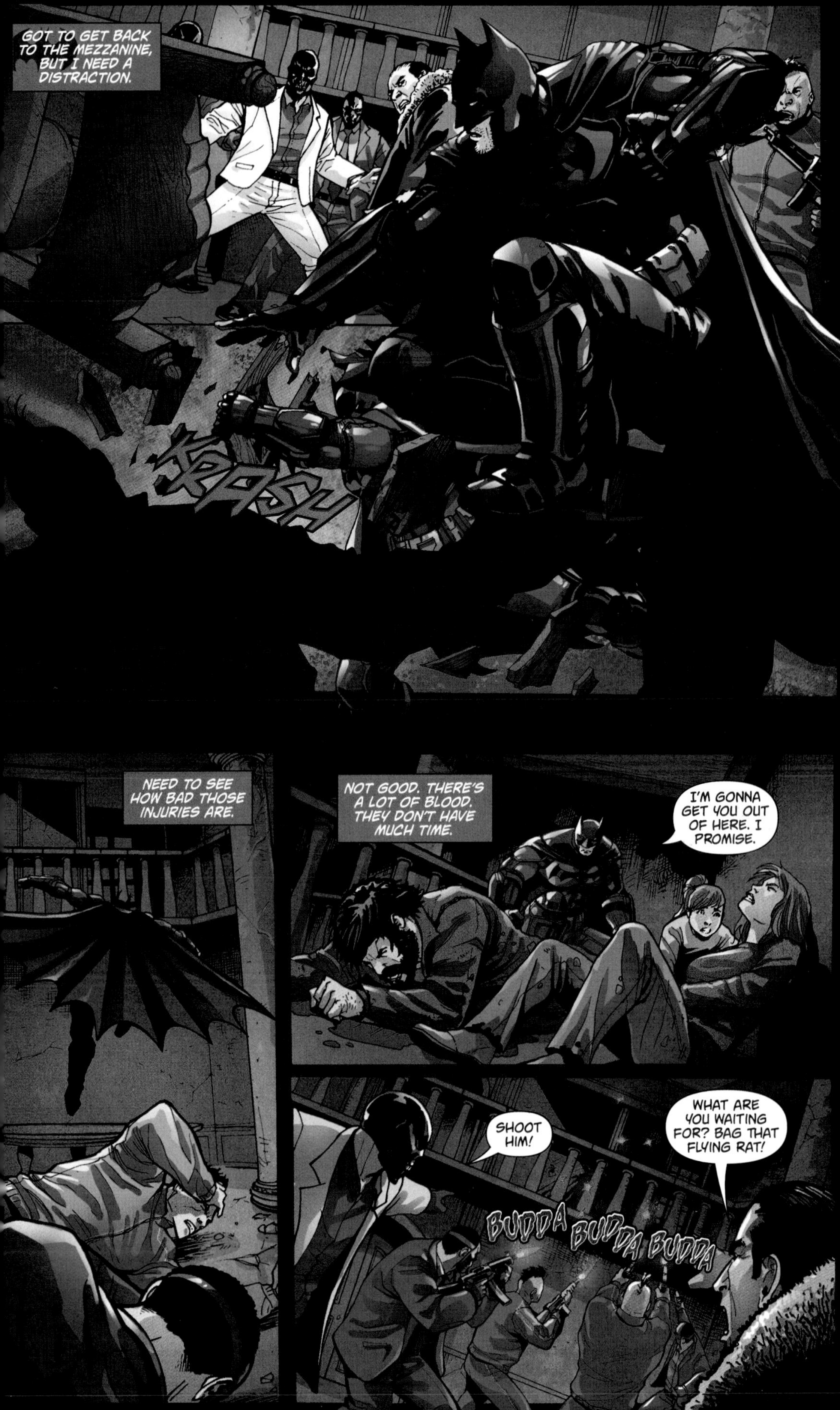
GOT TO GET BACK TO THE MEZZANINE, BUT I NEED A DISTRACTION.
KRASH
NEED TO SEE HOW BAD THOSE INJURIES ARE.
NOT GOOD. THERE'S A LOT OF BLOOD. THEY DON'T HAVE MUCH TIME.
I'M GONNA GET YOU OUT OF HERE. I PROMISE.
SHOOT HIM!
WHAT ARE YOU WAITING FOR? BAG THAT FLYING RAT!
BUDDA BUDDA BUDDA

I'M GONNA KILL YOU, PENGUIN! YOU HEAR ME? YOU'RE DEAD!

THERE! HE'S GETTING AWAY!

BOMB!

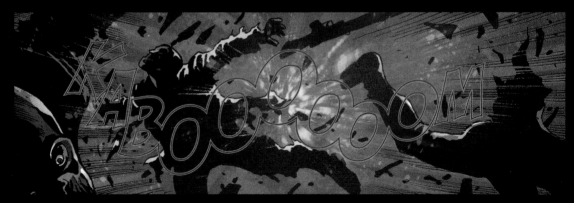

KABOOOOOOM

UGH

WHAT THE --?!

WAPP

THINGS ARE HEATING UP DOWN THERE. THIS CAN'T BE GOOD.

TO GO AFTER BLACK MASK AND PENGUIN, SKIP TO PAGE 136.
TO GEAR UP, SKIP TO PAGE 139.

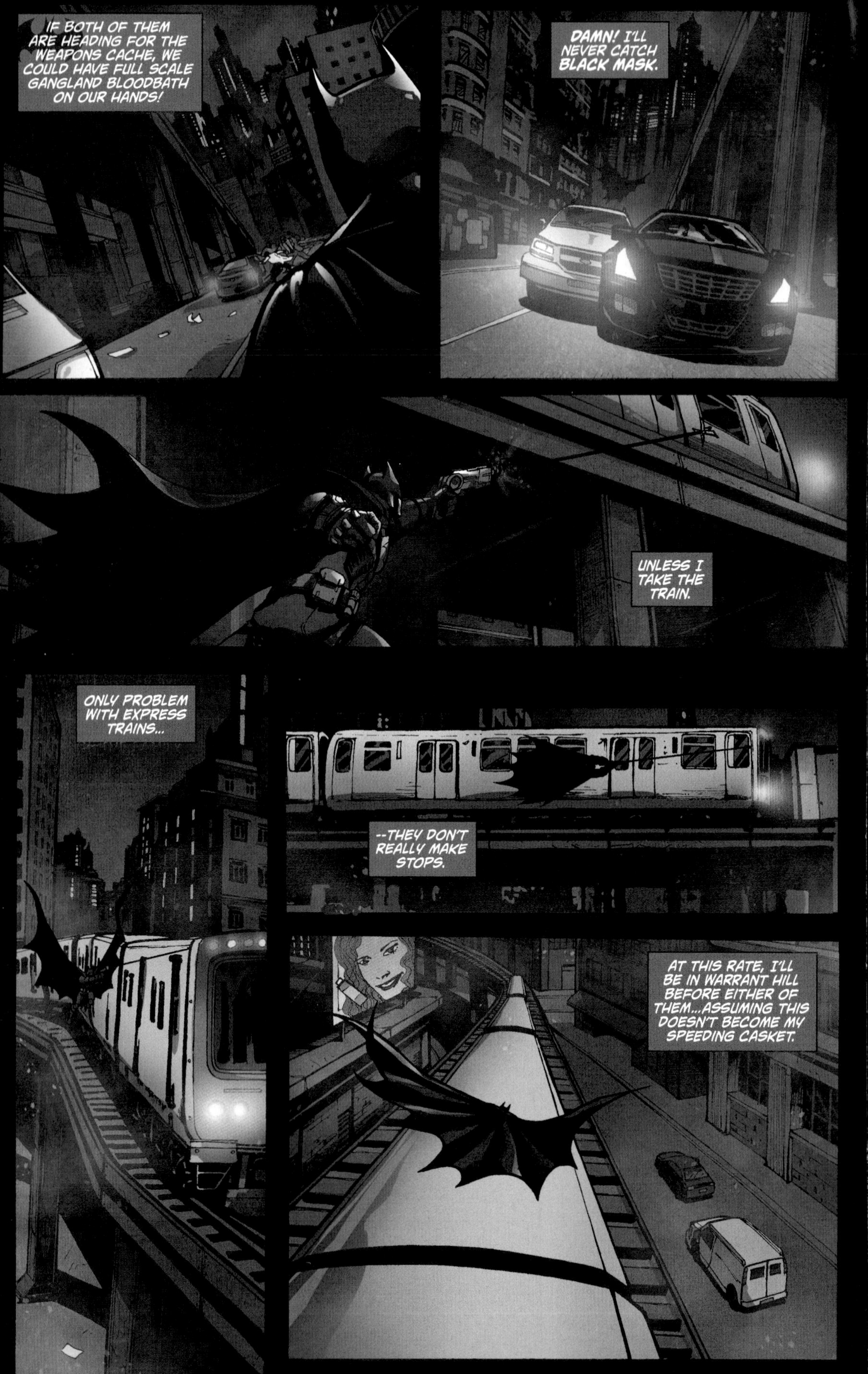
IF BOTH OF THEM ARE HEADING FOR THE WEAPONS CACHE, WE COULD HAVE FULL SCALE GANGLAND BLOODBATH ON OUR HANDS!
DAMN! I'LL NEVER CATCH BLACK MASK.
UNLESS I TAKE THE TRAIN.
ONLY PROBLEM WITH EXPRESS TRAINS...
--THEY DON'T REALLY MAKE STOPS.
AT THIS RATE, I'LL BE IN WARRANT HILL BEFORE EITHER OF THEM...ASSUMING THIS DOESN'T BECOME MY SPEEDING CASKET.

129

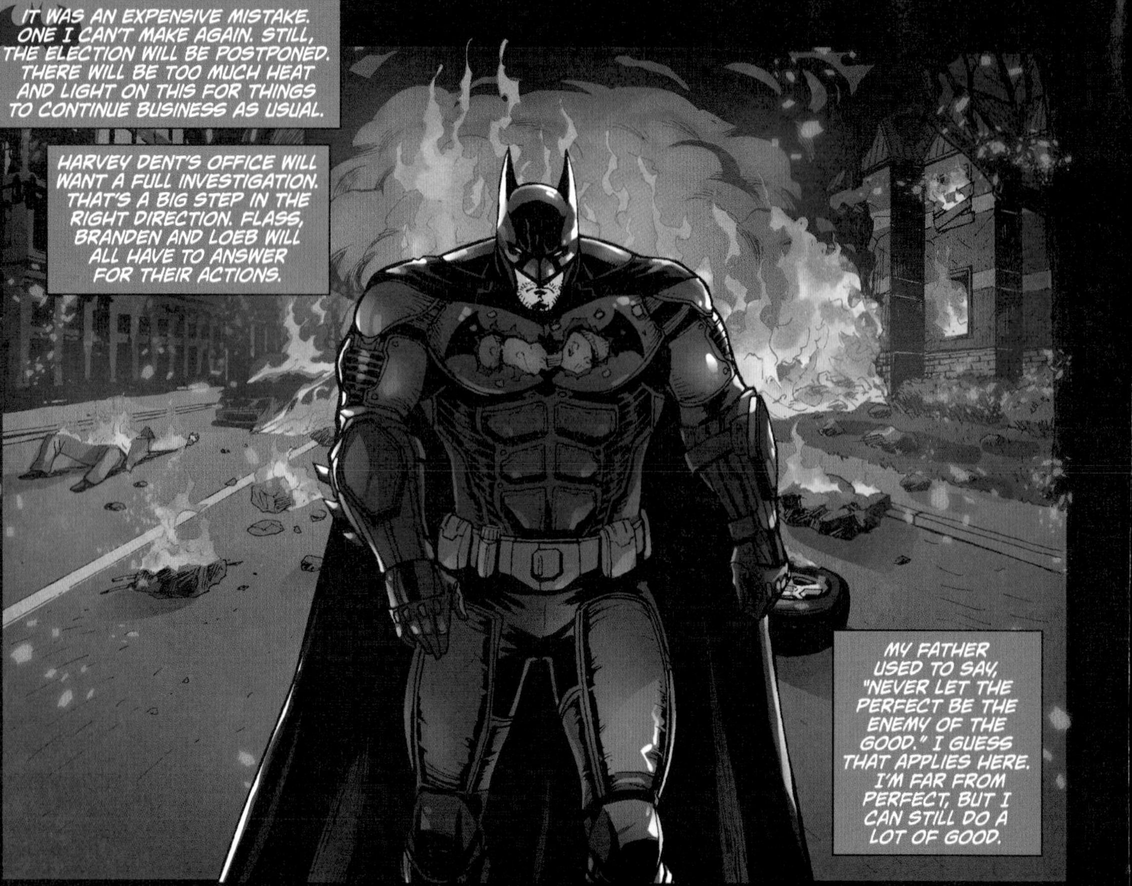
IT WAS AN EXPENSIVE MISTAKE. ONE I CAN'T MAKE AGAIN. STILL, THE ELECTION WILL BE POSTPONED. THERE WILL BE TOO MUCH HEAT AND LIGHT ON THIS FOR THINGS TO CONTINUE BUSINESS AS USUAL.
HARVEY DENT'S OFFICE WILL WANT A FULL INVESTIGATION. THAT'S A BIG STEP IN THE RIGHT DIRECTION. FLASS, BRANDEN AND LOEB WILL ALL HAVE TO ANSWER FOR THEIR ACTIONS.
MY FATHER USED TO SAY, "NEVER LET THE PERFECT BE THE ENEMY OF THE GOOD." I GUESS THAT APPLIES HERE. I'M FAR FROM PERFECT, BUT I CAN STILL DO A LOT OF GOOD.

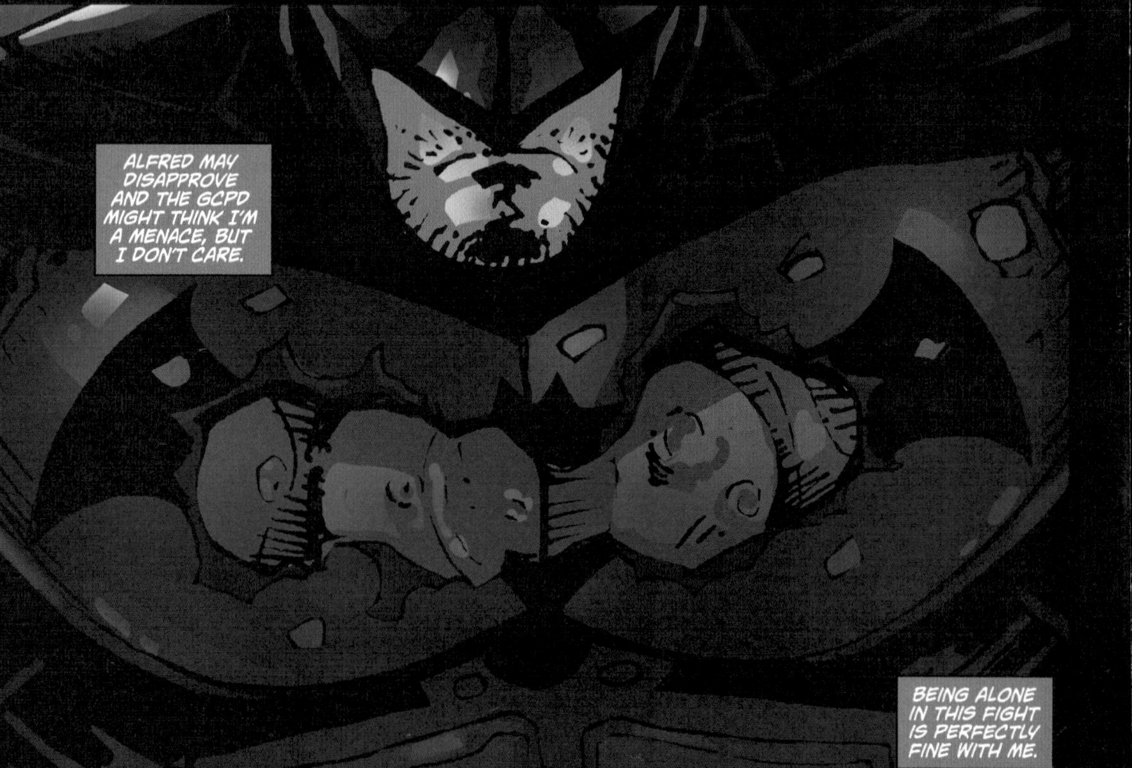
ALFRED MAY DISAPPROVE AND THE GCPD MIGHT THINK I'M A MENACE, BUT I DON'T CARE.
BEING ALONE IN THIS FIGHT IS PERFECTLY FINE WITH ME.

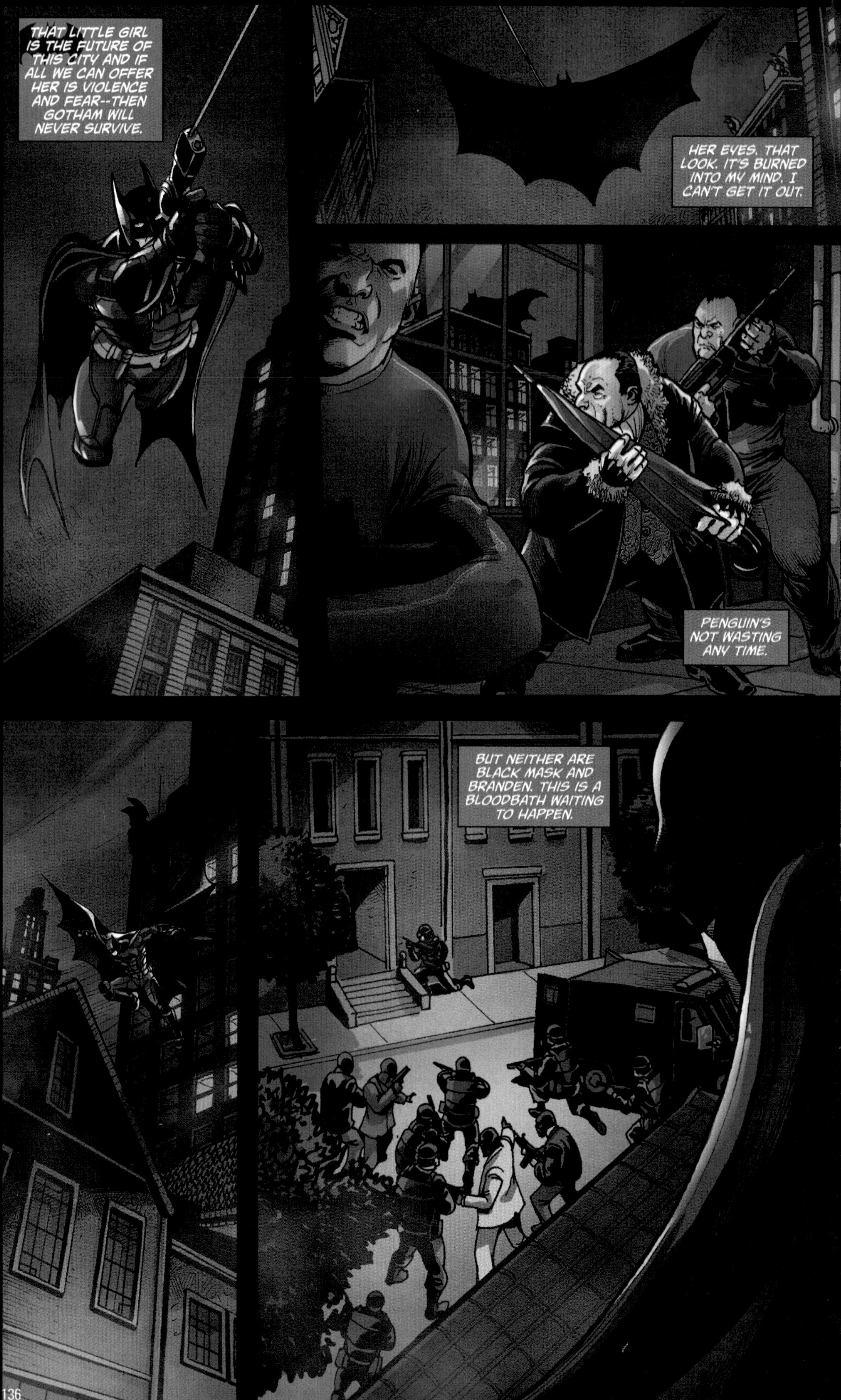
THAT LITTLE GIRL IS THE FUTURE OF THIS CITY AND IF ALL WE CAN OFFER HER IS VIOLENCE AND FEAR--THEN GOTHAM WILL NEVER SURVIVE.
HER EYES. THAT LOOK. IT'S BURNED INTO MY MIND. I CAN'T GET IT OUT.
PENGUIN'S NOT WASTING ANY TIME.
BUT NEITHER ARE BLACK MASK AND BRANDEN. THIS IS A BLOODBATH WAITING TO HAPPEN.

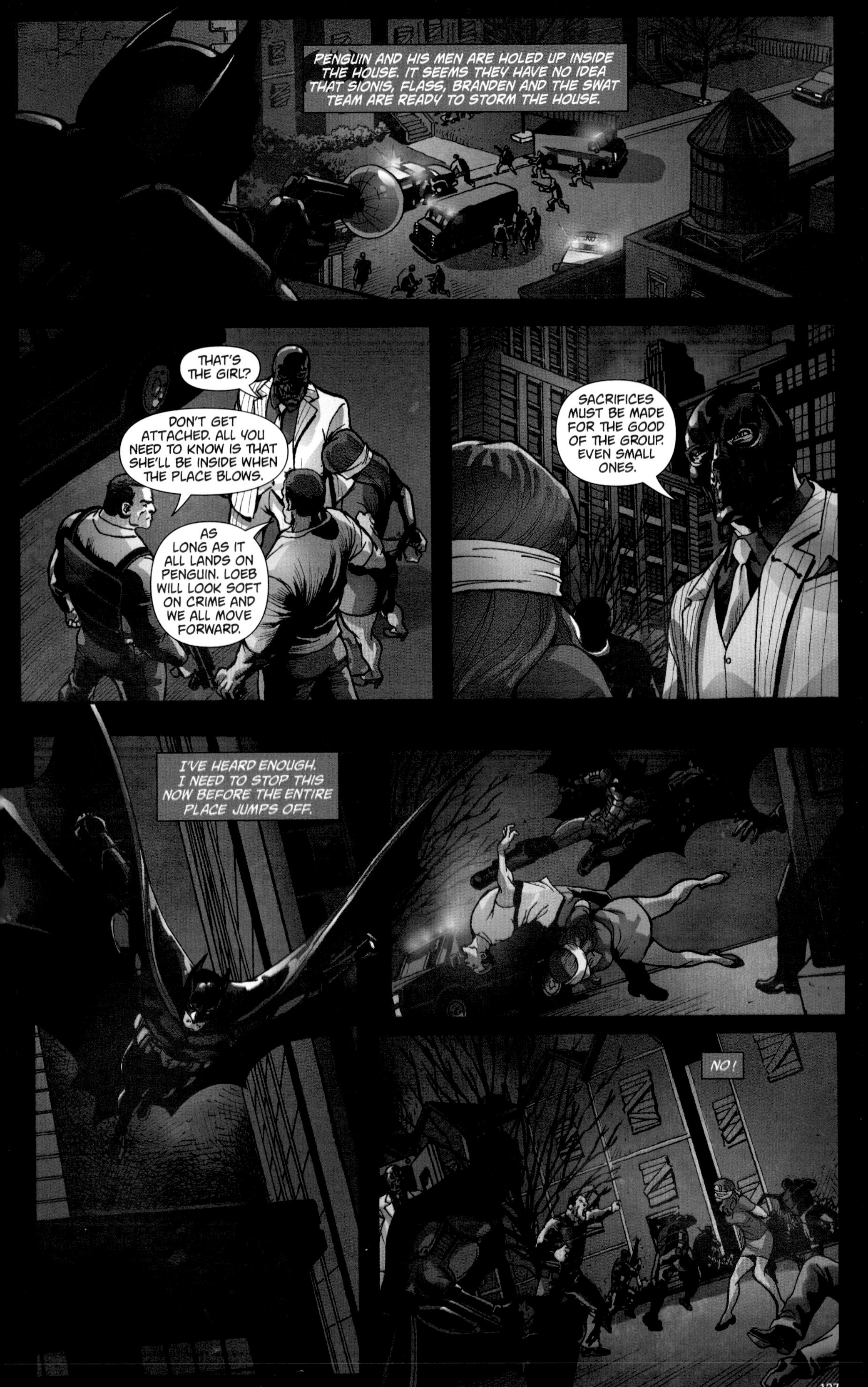
PENGUIN AND HIS MEN ARE HOLED UP INSIDE THE HOUSE. IT SEEMS THEY HAVE NO IDEA THAT SIONIS, FLASS, BRANDEN AND THE SWAT TEAM ARE READY TO STORM THE HOUSE.
THAT'S THE GIRL?
DON'T GET ATTACHED. ALL YOU NEED TO KNOW IS THAT SHE'LL BE INSIDE WHEN THE PLACE BLOWS.
AS LONG AS IT ALL LANDS ON PENGUIN. LOEB WILL LOOK SOFT ON CRIME AND WE ALL MOVE FORWARD.
SACRIFICES MUST BE MADE FOR THE GOOD OF THE GROUP. EVEN SMALL ONES.
I'VE HEARD ENOUGH. I NEED TO STOP THIS NOW BEFORE THE ENTIRE PLACE JUMPS OFF.
NO!

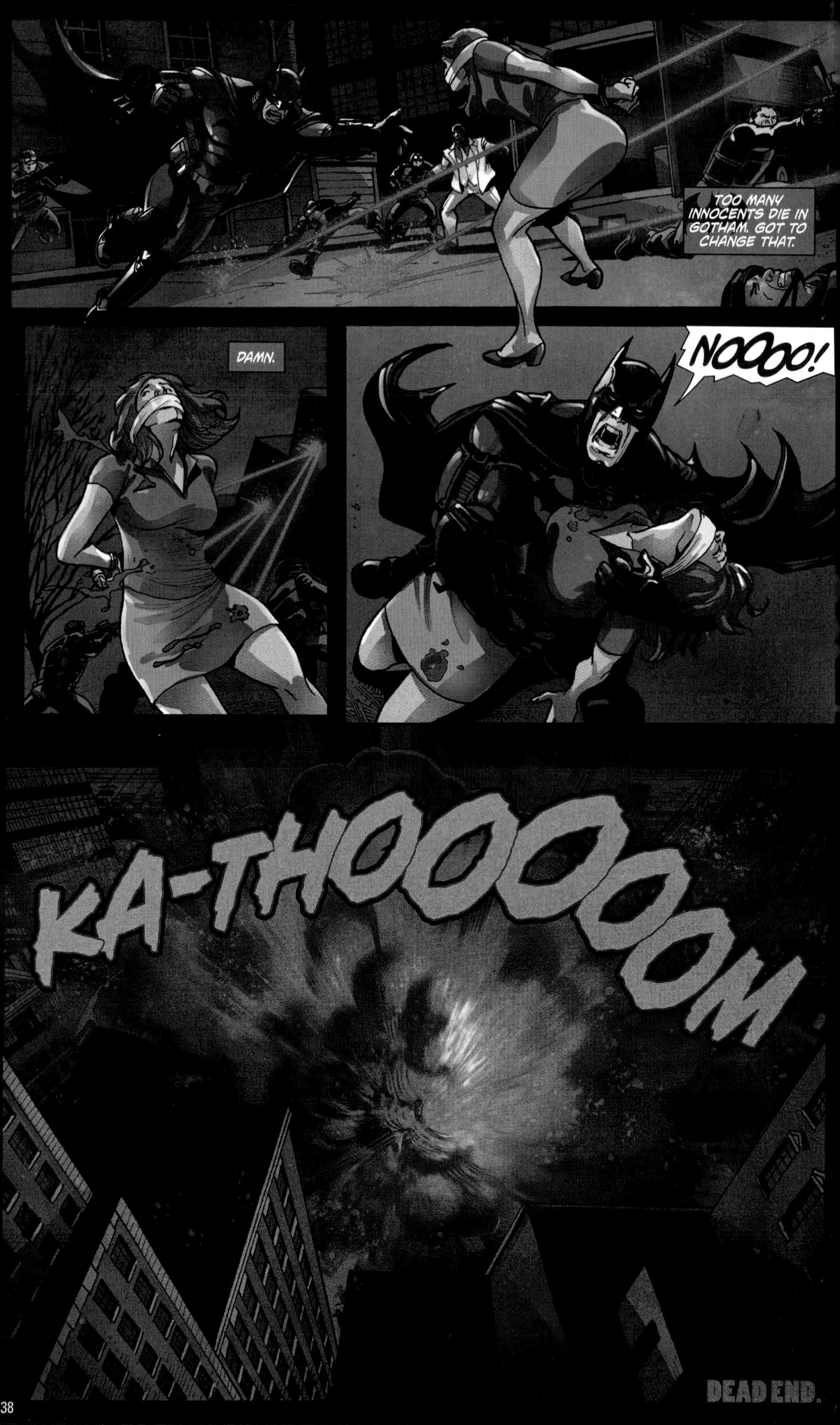
TOO MANY INNOCENTS DIE IN GOTHAM. GOT TO CHANGE THAT.
DAMN.
NOOOO!
KA-THOOOOOM
DEAD END.

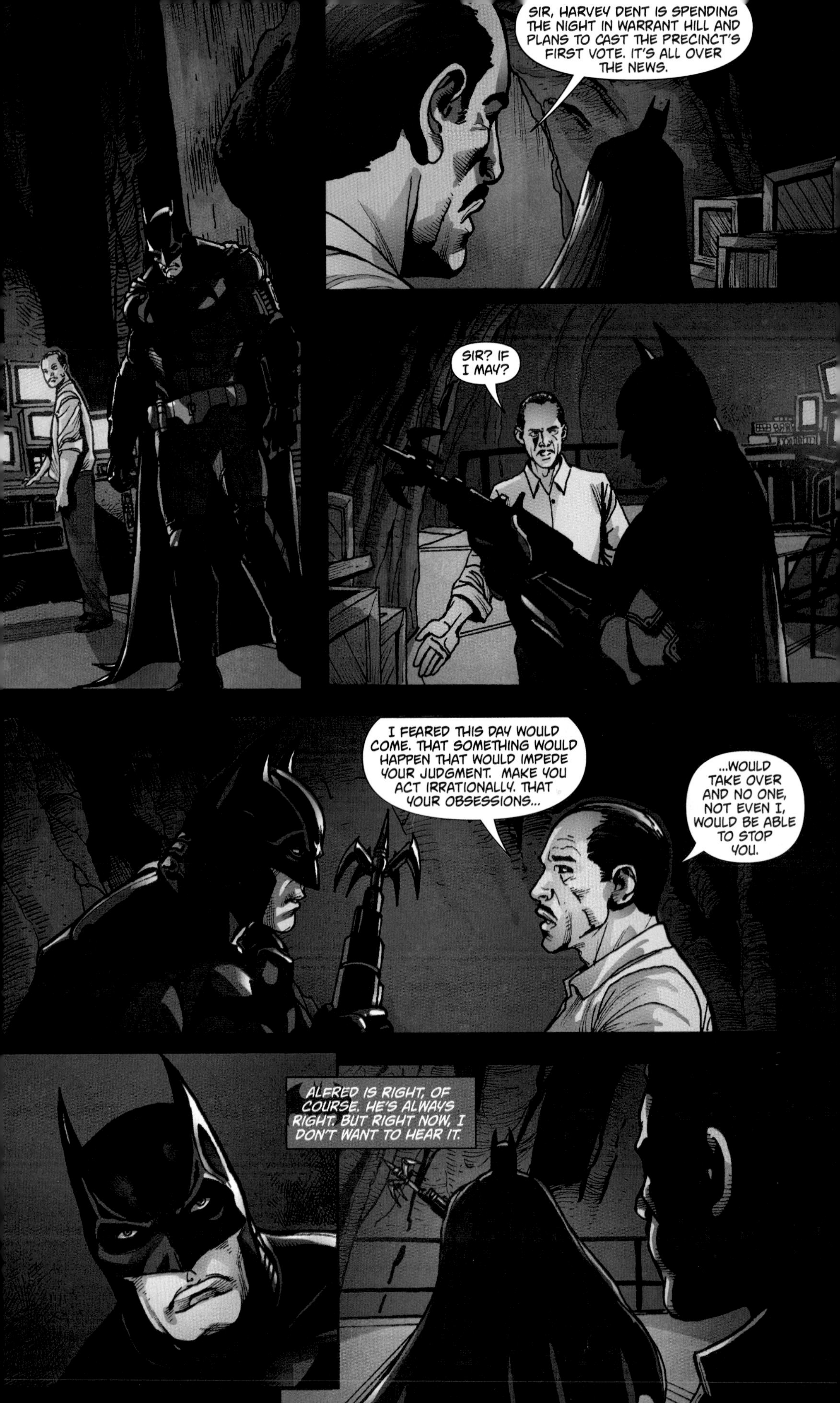

SIR, HARVEY DENT IS SPENDING THE NIGHT IN WARRANT HILL AND PLANS TO CAST THE PRECINCT'S FIRST VOTE. IT'S ALL OVER THE NEWS.
SIR? IF I MAY?
I FEARED THIS DAY WOULD COME. THAT SOMETHING WOULD HAPPEN THAT WOULD IMPEDE YOUR JUDGMENT. MAKE YOU ACT IRRATIONALLY. THAT YOUR OBSESSIONS...
...WOULD TAKE OVER AND NO ONE, NOT EVEN I, WOULD BE ABLE TO STOP YOU.
ALFRED IS RIGHT, OF COURSE. HE'S ALWAYS RIGHT. BUT RIGHT NOW, I DON'T WANT TO HEAR IT.

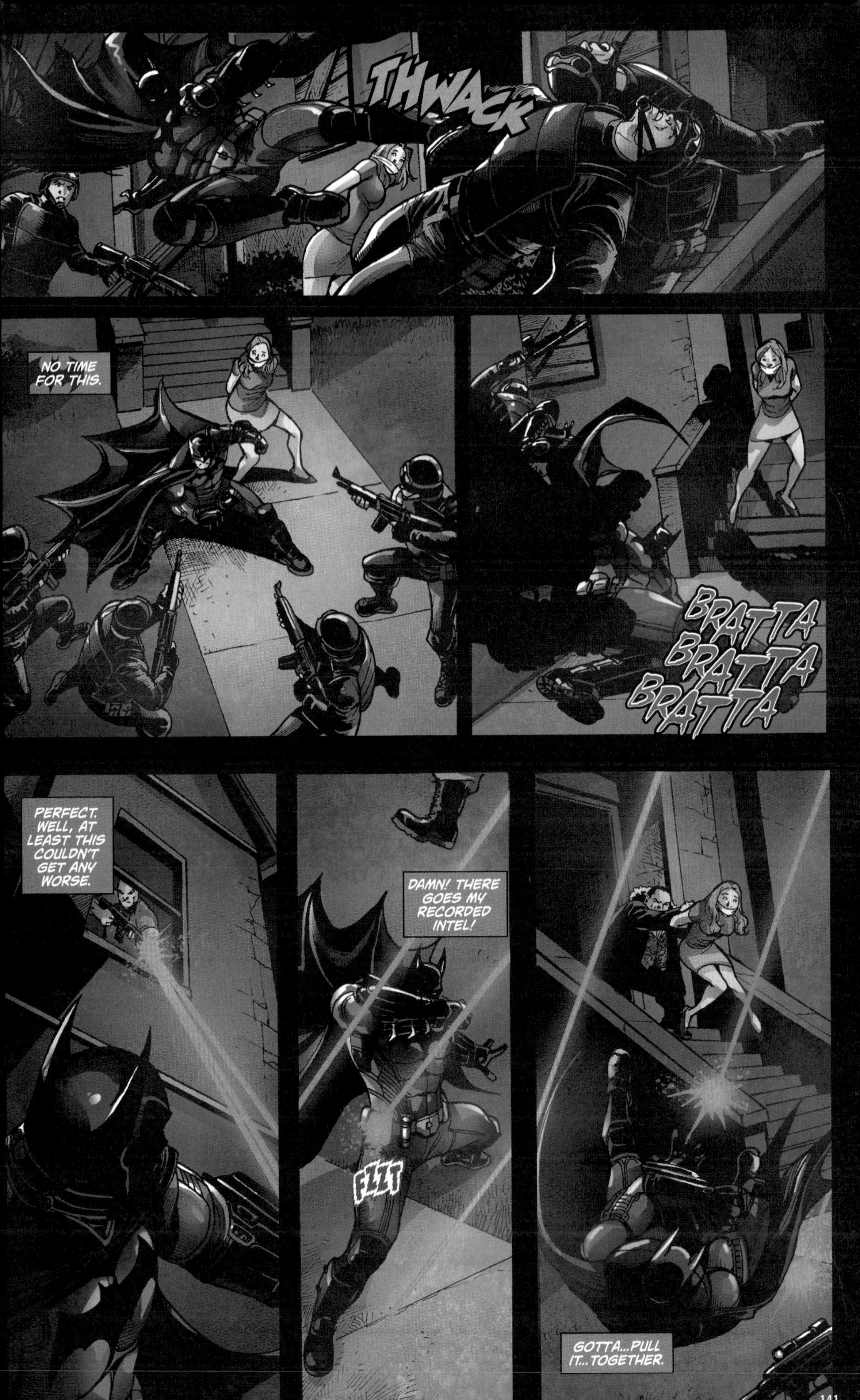
THWACK
NO TIME FOR THIS.
BRATTA BRATTA BRATTA
PERFECT. WELL, AT LEAST THIS COULDN'T GET ANY WORSE.
DAMN! THERE GOES MY RECORDED INTEL!
FLLT
GOTTA...PULL IT...TOGETHER.

THE NEXT DAY...

YOU'VE GOT TO BE KIDDING ME!

AFTER A SHOOT OUT IN WARRANT HILL THAT LED TO THE DISCOVERY OF A HOUSE FILLED WITH EXPLOSIVES, THE CITY MADE AN EMERGENCY DECISION TO DELAY ELECTION PROCEEDINGS...

...UNTIL A FULL INVESTIGATION BY DISTRICT ATTORNEY HARVEY DENT CAN BE CONCLUDED.

SHOOT OUT

...NG SHOOT OUT IN W

SOURCES CLOSE TO THE INVESTIGATION TELL GOTHAM NEWS FIVE THAT ALLEGATIONS OF CORRUPTION INSIDE THE GCPD ARE CENTRAL TO THE DA'S CASE...

...CASE AND IS SET TO WIDEN TO OTHER AREAS OF CITY GOVERNMENT.

I SHOULD'VE TAKEN THEM ALL DOWN DIRECTLY.

STILL, I SUPPOSE THE SUSPENSION OF THE ELECTION KEEPS THE CITY OUT OF THEIR HANDS.

FOR NOW...

SHOOT OUT

...OUT IN WAR...LL

FOR ALFRED, THE CHOICE TO STOP SEEMS SIMPLE. HE FEELS A NEED TO PROTECT ME.

BUT YOU KNOW THEY'LL TRY AGAIN--AS, I FEAR, WILL YOU. IT'S A ZERO-SUM GAME, MASTER BRUCE. I DON'T LIKE YOUR CHANCES.

I DO...

FOR ME, IT'S ALSO SIMPLE. MY NEED TO PROTECT THE CITY IS WHAT DRIVES ME AND THAT'S SOMETHING MUCH BIGGER AND MORE IMPORTANT THAN I'LL EVER BE.

END.

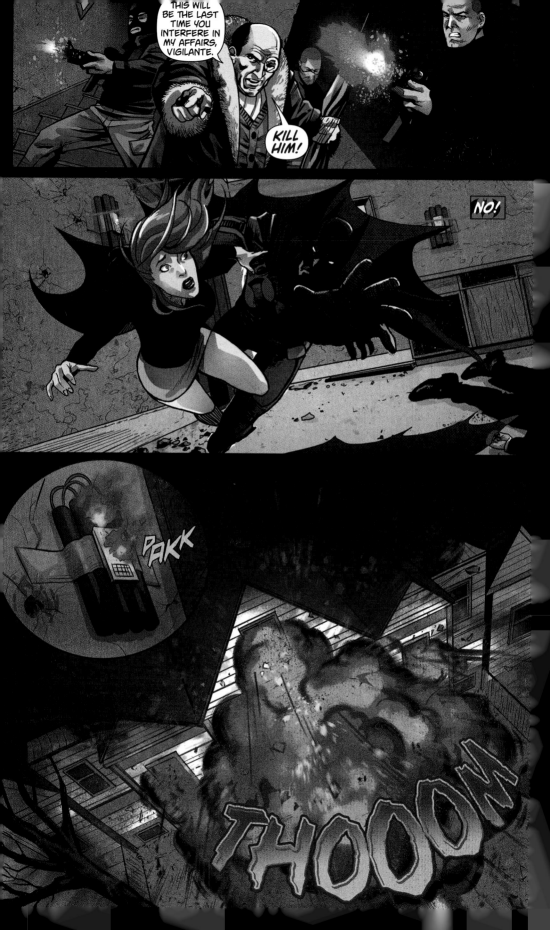

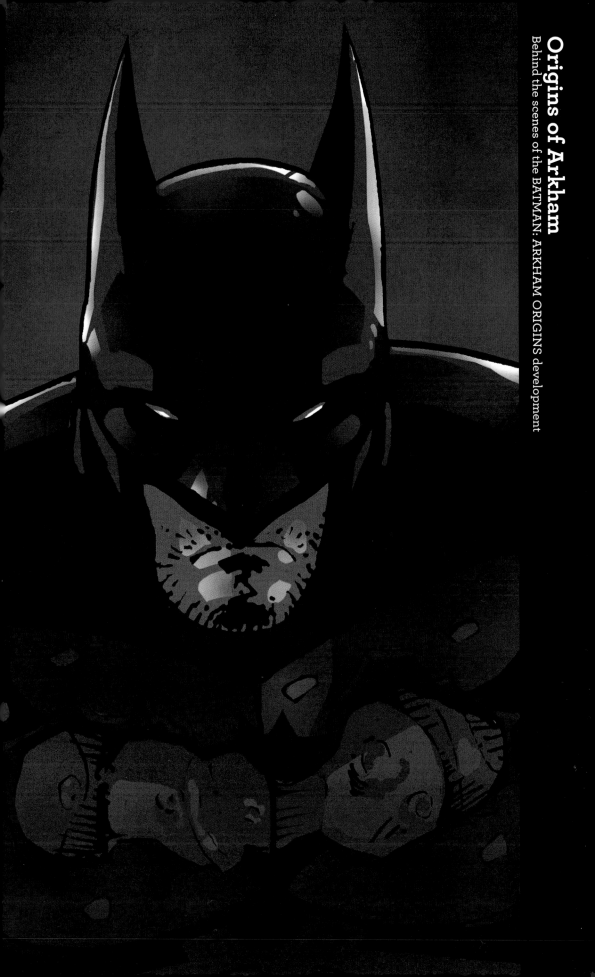

Origins of Arkham

Behind the scenes of the BATMAN: ARKHAM ORIGINS development

DC² MULTIVERSE

ARKHAM ORIGINS ROADMAP

X = Dead End

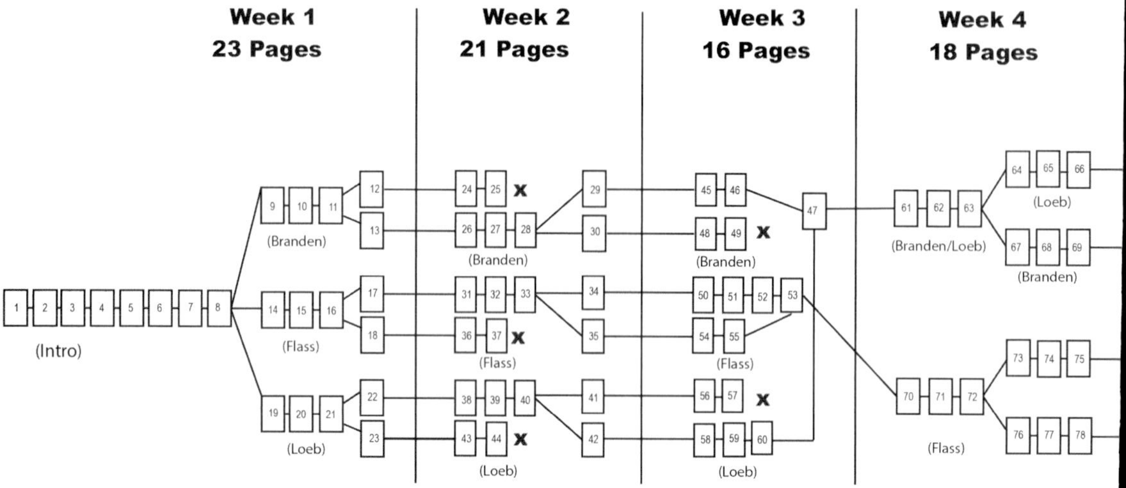
Week 1
23 Pages
Week 2
21 Pages
Week 3
16 Pages
Week 4
18 Pages
1 2 3 4 5 6 7 8
(Intro)
9 10 11 12 13
(Branden)
14 15 16 17 18
(Flass)
19 20 21 22 23
(Loeb)
24 25 X
26 27 28
(Branden)
29 30
31 32 33 34 35
36 37 X
(Flass)
38 39 40 41 42
43 44 X
(Loeb)
45 46 47
48 49 X
(Branden)
50 51 52 53
54 55
(Flass)
56 57 X
58 59 60
(Loeb)
61 62 63
(Branden/Loeb)
64 65 66
(Loeb)
67 68 69
(Branden)
70 71 72
(Flass)
73 74 75
76 77 78

Here is the roadmap created by the editors to help outline the progress and development of the story.

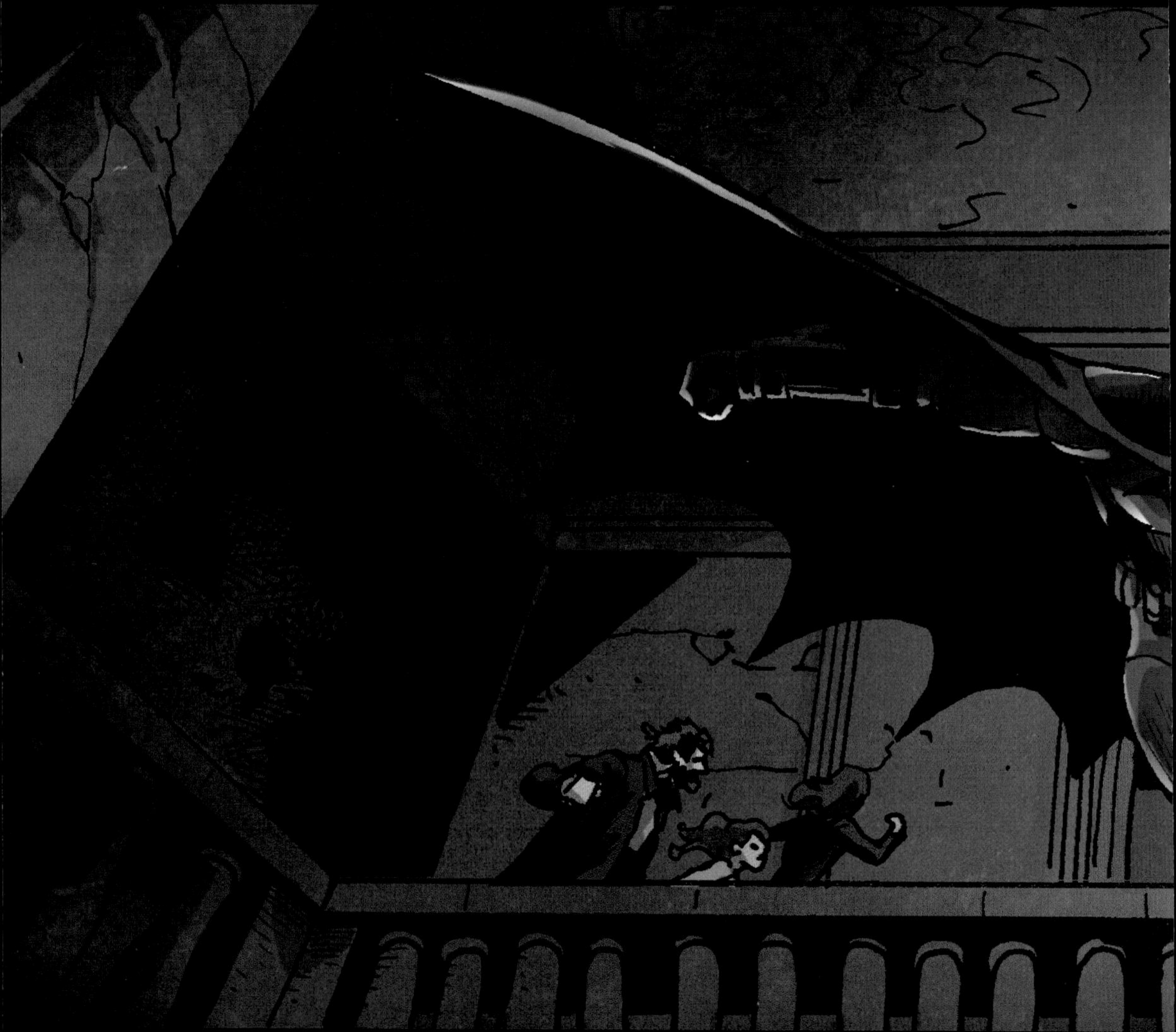

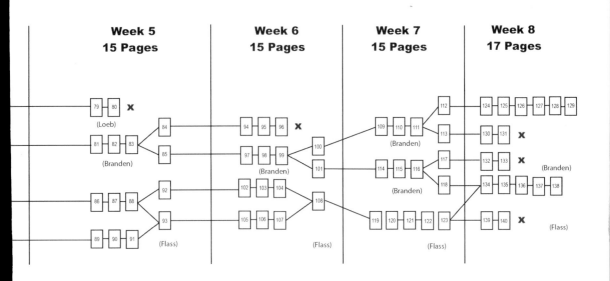

For the digital release of the story, there were many panels that had multiple versions drawn in order to properly animate the story. The following are examples of those panels. Page 23

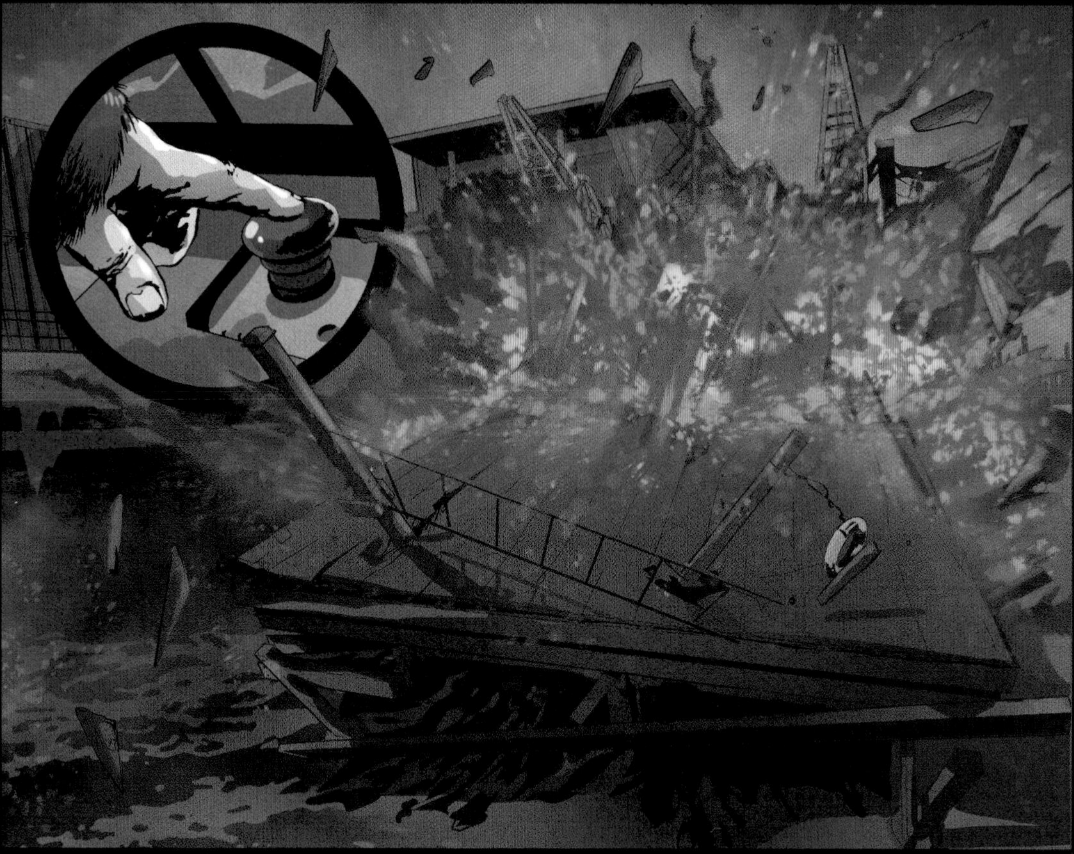

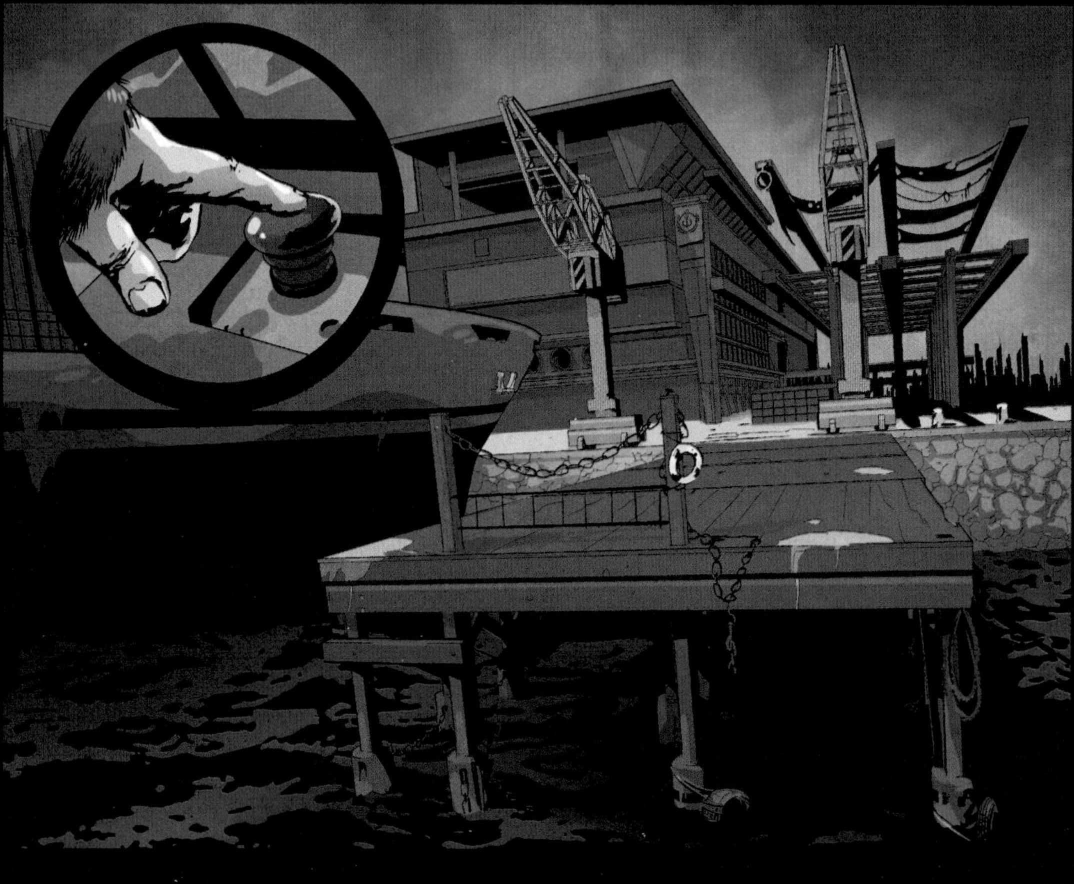

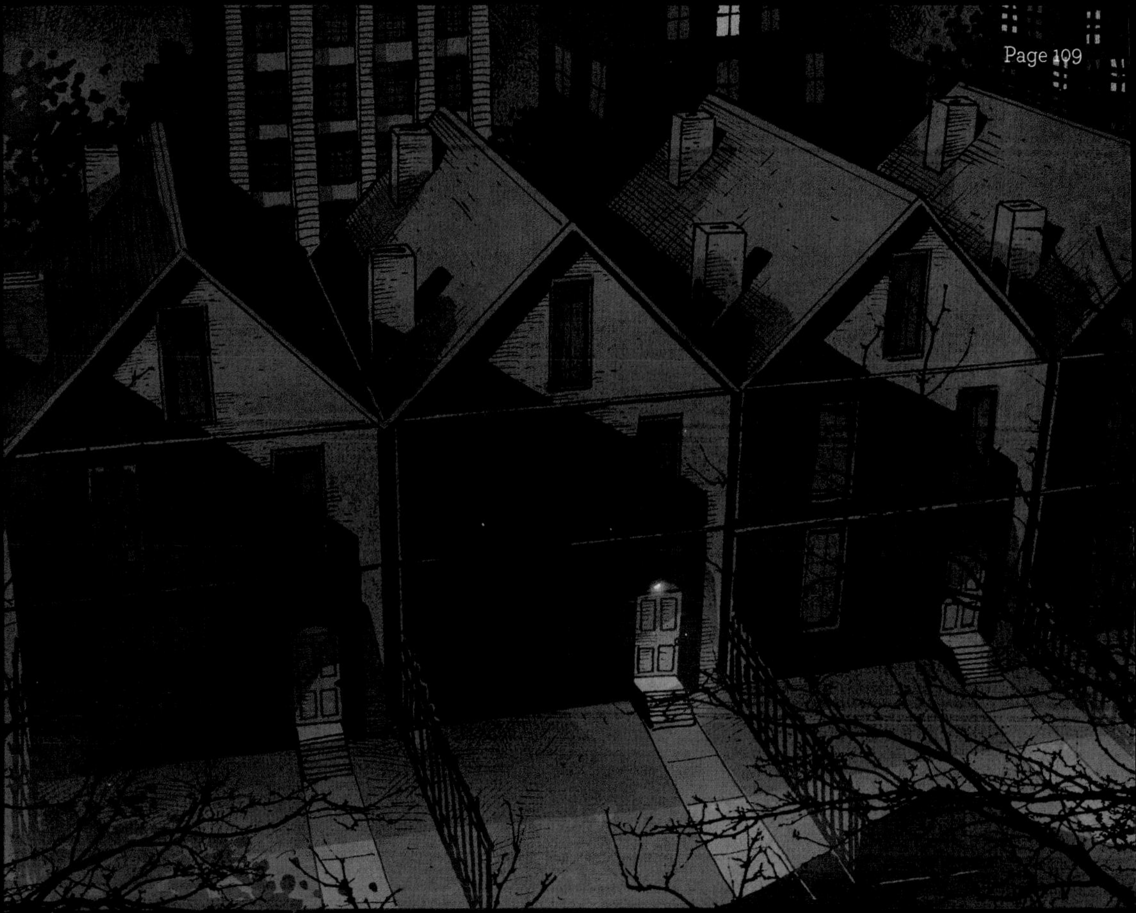

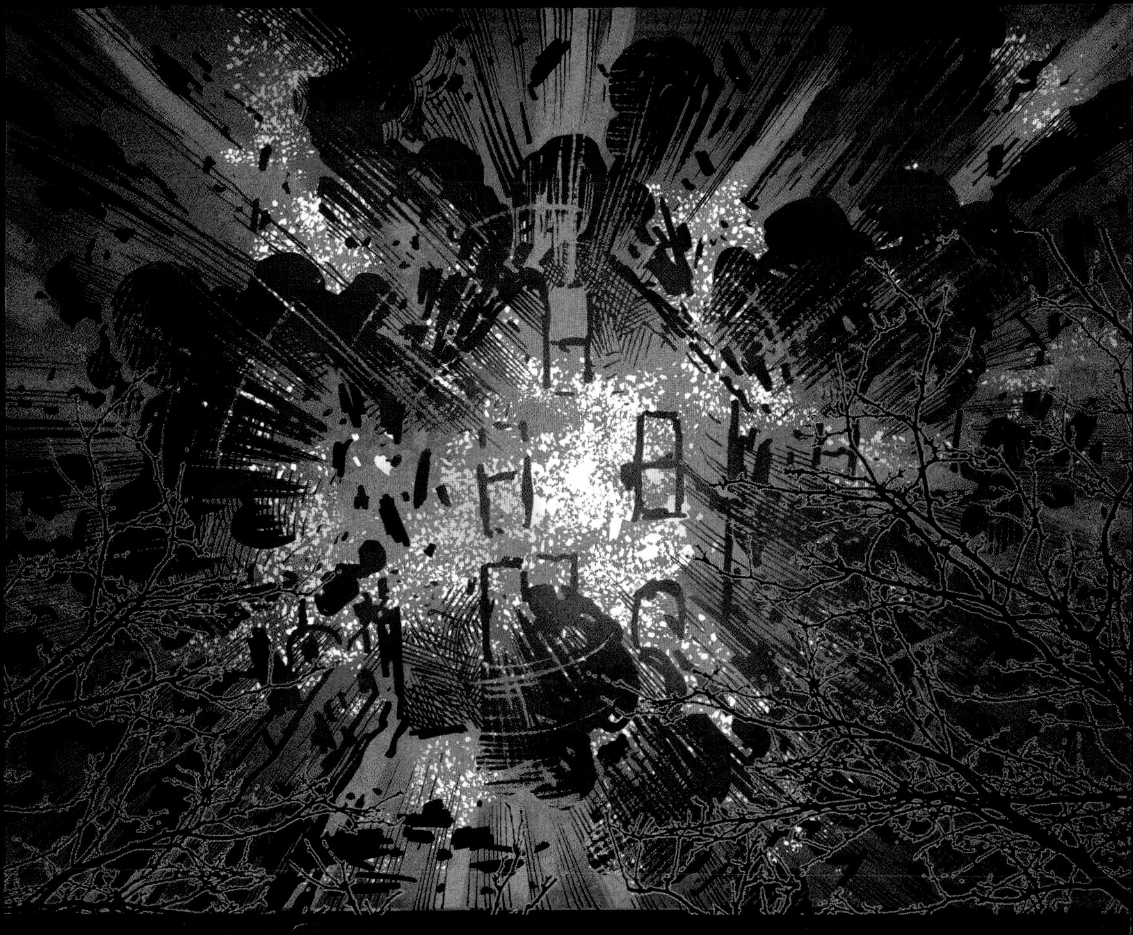

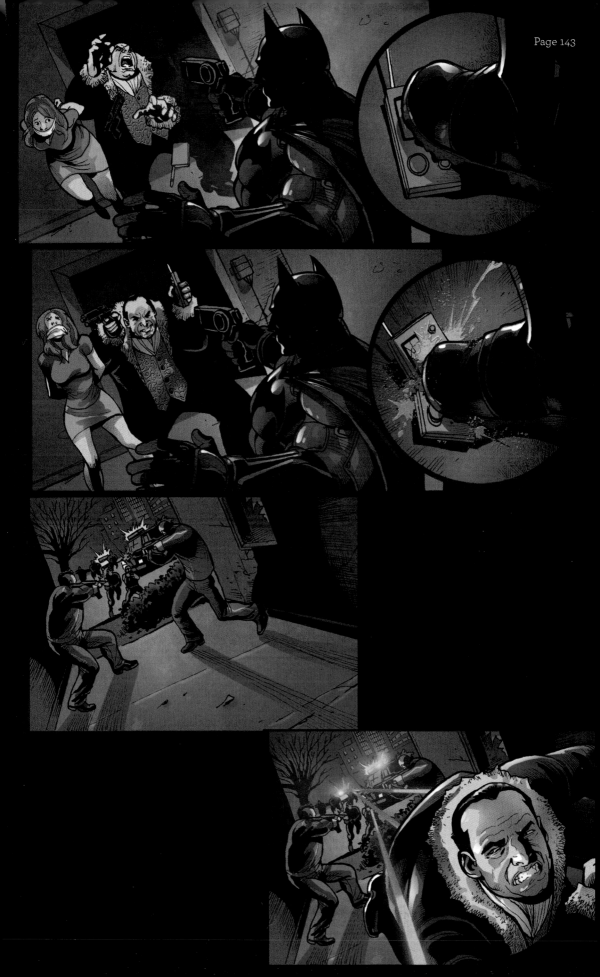

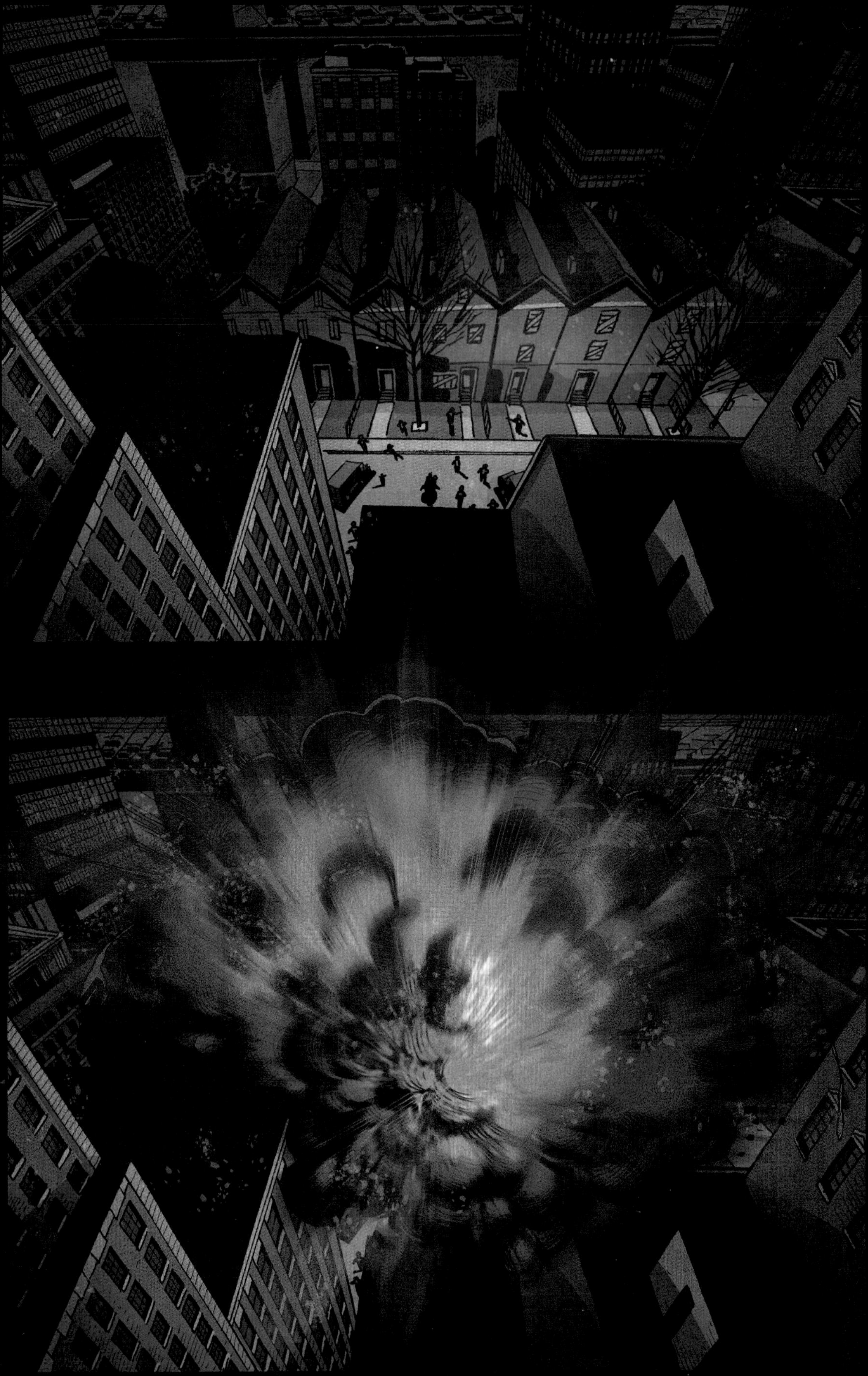

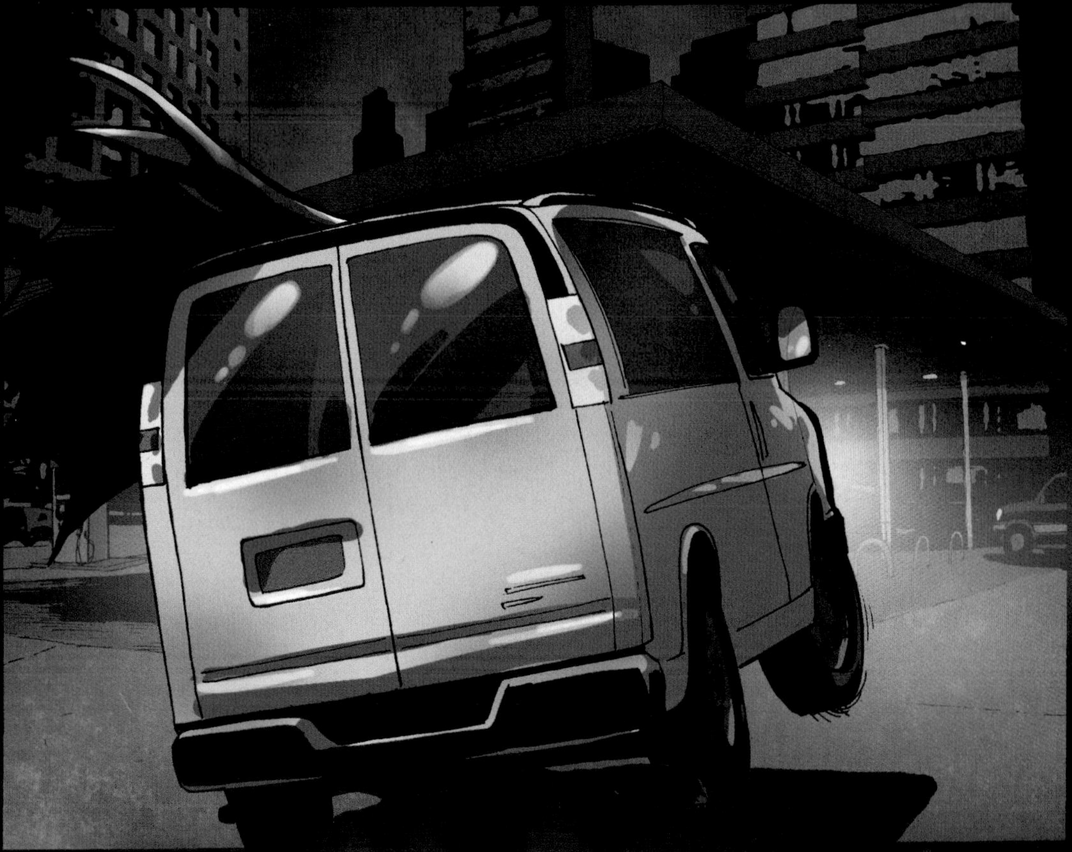

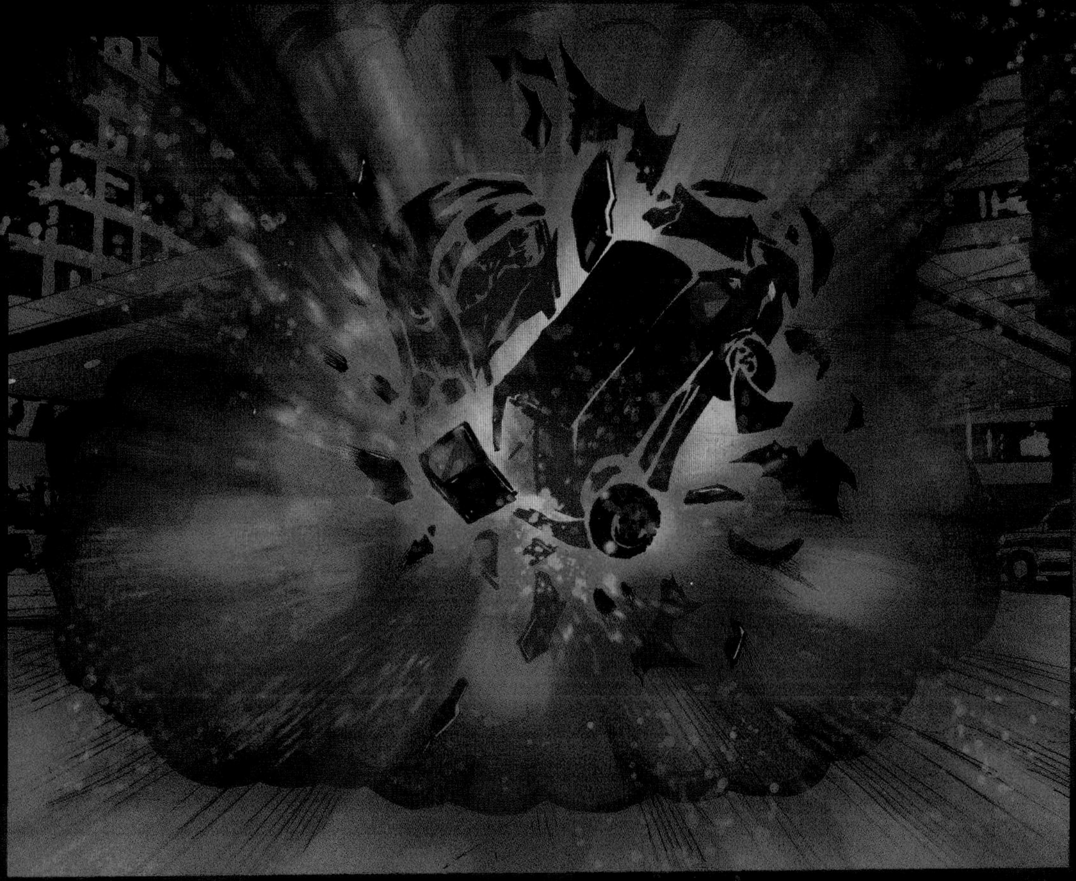

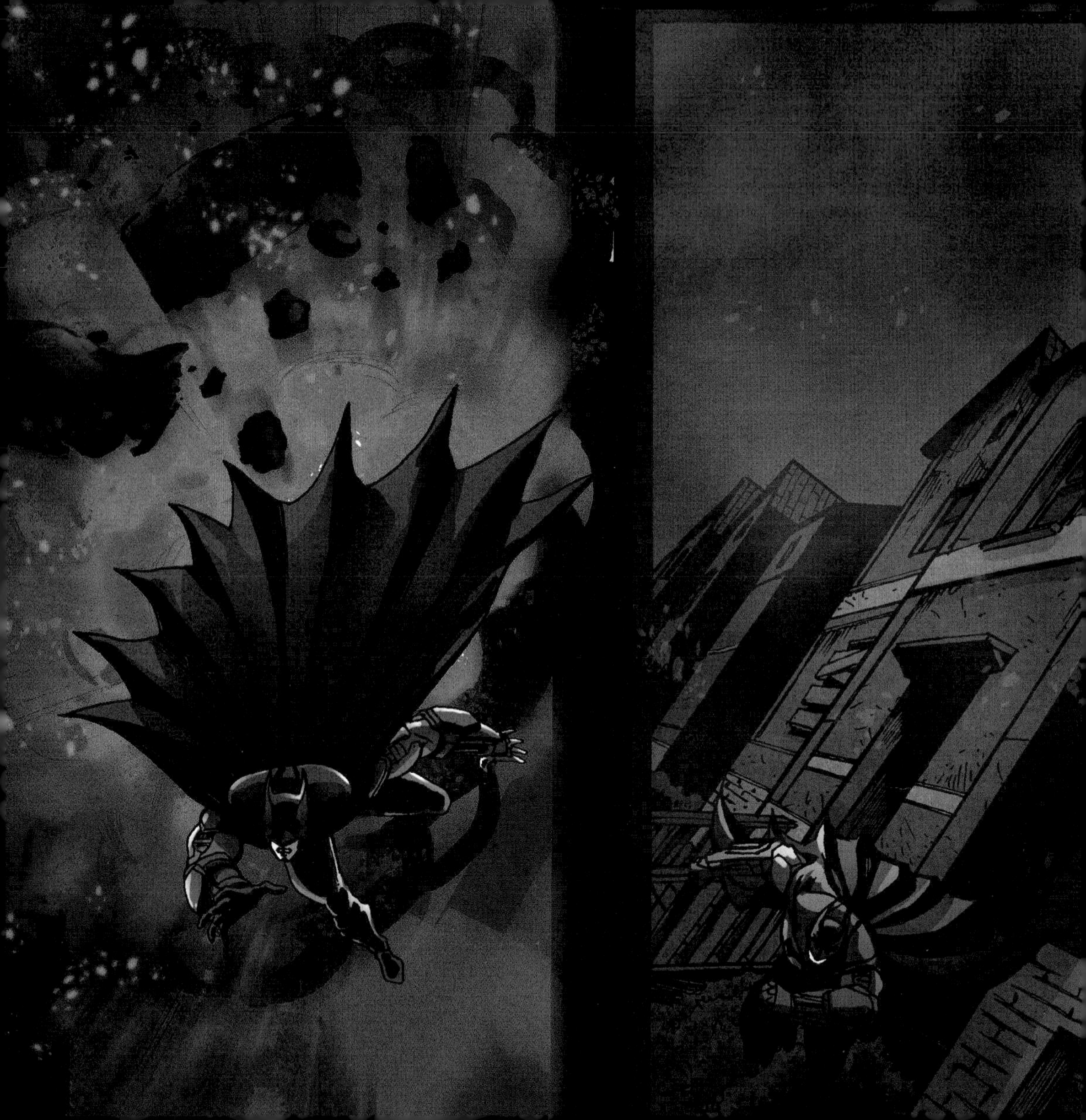

DC
COMICS™

GRANT MORRISON
with FRANK QUITELY

FINAL CRISIS

with J.G. JONES, CARLOS PACHECO & DOUG MAHNKE

BATMAN:
ARKHAM ASYLUM

with DAVE McKEAN

SEVEN SOLDIERS OF
VICTORY VOLS. 1 & 2

with J.H. WILLIAMS III &
VARIOUS ARTISTS

ALL ★ STAR

SUPERMAN

GRANT MORRISON
FRANK QUITELY
JAMIE GRANT

DC
COMICS